# 50 DOG SNACK RECIPES

*Holiday Gift Ideas and Homemade Dog Treats*

*(Dog Training and Dog Care Series - Book 3)*

Vikk Simmons

## Copyright Information

*50 Dog Snack Recipes: Holiday Gift Ideas and Homemade Dog Treats (Dog Training and Dog Care Series, Book 3)*

©2015 Vikk Simmons
All rights reserved worldwide. No part of this book may be reproduced in any form whatsoever, without the prior written permission of the publisher, except in case of brief quotations embodied in critical reviews and certain other noncommercial uses permitted by copyright law.

**NOTICE** - Readers are urged to seek the advice of their veterinarians before feeding their dogs any homemade food, including the recipes found in this book. These recipes are for treats and snacks and are not meant to replace any dog's normal and regular diet. While most dogs tolerate the food prepared from these recipes, there are dogs that have food allergies and other food intolerances. The author and the publisher cannot be held for any resulting problems.

Cover: Cathy Stucker

Ordinary Publishing Matters
www.OrdinaryMattersPublishing.com

Printed in the United States of America
1st print edition: December 2015

More Books in the Dog Training and Care Series
*Bonding with Your Rescue Dog: Decoding and Influencing Dog Behavior: A Gentle Approach to Understanding and Influencing Canine Behavior*
*Easy Homemade Dog Treat Recipes: Fun Homemade Dog Treats for the Busy Pet Lover*
Visit: http://www.alifewithdogs.com

## Thank-you Gift

I'm delighted that you have purchased *50 DOG SNACK RECIPES: Holiday Gift Ideas and Homemade Dog Treats*. As a thank-you, here is your bonus gift. Grab your 27-page free Dog Training and Resource Guide now.

http://www.alifewithdogs.com/a-life-with-dogs-free-gift/

Great for puppies, new dogs, and as a refresher for all other dogs.

## Praise for *Easy Homemade Dog Treat Recipes*

"*I am impressed by the wealth of information . . . this book would be a great resource for any dog owner, your dog will love you for it.*" — ML Fitz (Amazon)

"*I learned a lot of important DO's and DON'Ts when it comes to healthy feeding of the pets we love*". — Dan DeFigio (Amazon)

"*This book is a must be read for any dog owner.*" — Midge (Amazon)

## Praise for *Bonding with Your Rescue Dog*

"*Highly recommended to all dog lovers as well as those considering adopting a dog!*" — Anne (Amazon)

*This book details what will be needed after you pick your new pet, how to look after them, what to expect from them, and of course, how to bond with them.*" — Amy Ryan (Amazon)

"*— a must for first time owners and should be read by everyone thinking of adopting a new dog.*" — Walter Kane (Amazon)

"*A very enjoyable book to read and very well written.*" — Lysanne P. (Amazon)

"*Useful information about dog behaviors (and how to change them.)* — Cathy Stucker (Amazon Vine)

# Foreword

I confess to being a spoiler. I'm sure my friends say I spoil my dogs. What dog owner doesn't have the same desire? Not only is it relaxing to create a batch of dog treats, biscuits, or cookies that set all my dogs drooling, it's an activity I can share with the dogs. When that aroma of homemade biscuits fills the room, it's inevitable: the dogs drool. Love how their big, bright eyes watch me, all the while with them quietly waiting. Once biscuits are in hand, they line up, crowding each other for space, wiggling and shoving, nudging and nuzzling until they see their prize coming toward them.

I'm delighted at the response to *Easy Homemade Treat Recipes: Fun Homemade Treats for the Busy Pet Lover*. So many readers have told me how much they enjoy making treats for their dogs, too. Because of their kind words, I wanted to share even more treats. So I began writing and compiling with the aim of creating a fun party and holiday themed recipe book. This has been a rewarding project. You'll find many of these recipes will also make perfect gifts for your friends and family. Stash them in tins, keep them in zip lock bags, and share them with other dog-friendly family members and friends. You do give your dogs presents, right? I know we do.

To receive updates and notices of my new books, be sure and favorite me on my Amazon author page, visit the A Life with Dogs Facebook fan page, and join my list of VIP readers.

Enjoy,

Vikk Simmons

*Vikk Simmons*

## About 50 Dog Snack Recipes

Let's face it, you love your dog. Your dog is your best friend and companion – shouldn't you treat him as such? I know mine are my best buddies and daily companions. Today some would call me a "pet parent." Given that many experts say dogs have the intelligence and behavior of toddlers, I guess I fit right in there.

Pet parents all around the world pamper their pooches with fancy beds, cute outfits, and special toys but you do not have to spend a fortune to indulge your dog. I know I don't have that kind of money. If you're like me, you are happy to find inexpensive ways to keep your dog happy. Let's face it. Spending time with your dog is all he really wants, but, trust me, he won't say no to a tasty treat now and then.

Have you walked the aisles of your favorite pet store? You're probably overwhelmed at the selection. Dog treats come in all kinds of flavors but if you buy them at the pet store you might be surprised at the high price for those high-quality treats. As an alternative, have you ever considered making some of your own homemade dog biscuits and treats?

By making your own dog treats you have control over what ingredients you use and you can customize your treats to suit your dog's individual preferences for flavor.

In this book you will find a collection of fifty-plus wonderful recipes for homemade dog biscuits and treats suitable for your own dog or given as gifts to other pet parents and their dogs. These recipes include a wide variety of ingredients that are healthy for dogs including yogurt, peanut butter, whole-wheat flour, carob, and more. With so many recipes to choose from you will never run out of ideas and you can try several recipes to see which ones your dog likes best. I bet you find you end up envying your dog when you see the look in his eyes as he stares fixedly at the biscuit you are offering.

As I said, not only can you use the recipes in this book to make homemade treats and biscuits for your own dog, but you can also make them for your friends and family! Homemade dog treats and biscuits are a fun and thoughtful gift that any dog owner would be glad to receive. As an added bonus, many of the recipes in this book are holiday-themed so they are great gifts for dog lovers during the holiday season. Even those recipes that are not specifically holiday-themed, however, can still be given as gifts.

If you are ready to give homemade dog biscuits and treats a try, simply pick a recipe and get started!

*Dogs are not our whole life,
but they make our lives whole.*

Roger Caras

*My fashion philosophy is, if you're not covered with
dog hair, your life is empty.*

Elayne Boosier

*50 Dog Snack Recipes*

# Table of Contents

**FOREWORD** ............................................................................. 5
**ABOUT 50 DOG SNACK RECIPES** ........................................... 7
**TABLE OF CONTENTS** ............................................................ 11
**INTRODUCTION** ..................................................................... 15
    A WORD OF CAUTION ............................................................... 16
**HOLIDAY GIFT IDEAS USING TREAT JARS** ............................ 17
    DIY TREAT JAR LIDS ................................................................ 18
    FUN DIY TREAT BAGS ............................................................. 18
    QUICK DIY DOG COLLAR TREAT JAR ..................................... 19
    SUPER EASY DYI DOG TREAT JAR .......................................... 19
**HOLIDAY GIFT IDEAS USING WREATHS** ............................... 21
    DIY EASY DOG BISCUIT CHRISTMAS WREATH ........................ 23
    DIY HOMEMADE DOG BONE WREATH ................................... 24
**BEWARE OF HIDDEN HOLIDAY DANGERS** ........................... 27
    POINSETTIAS, MISTLETOE, AND HOLLY ................................... 27
    CHRISTMAS CAKE, MINCE PIES, AND CHRISTMAS PUDDING ... 27
    CHOCOLATE DECORATIONS, CHOCOLATE COINS ..................... 28
    MACADAMIA NUTS AND WALNUTS ......................................... 28
    BONES ..................................................................................... 29
    ALCOHOL ................................................................................. 29
    WHAT YOU CAN DO ................................................................ 29
**TIPS TO KEEP YOUR DOG SAFE DURING THE HOLIDAYS** ... 30
**MAKING HOMEMADE DOG SNACKS** ..................................... 31
    THREE GOLDEN RULES FOR MAKING HOMEMADE DOG TREATS .... 35
    THE HEALTH BENEFITS OF HOMEMADE DOG TREATS ............... 36
    HOW MANY TREATS IS TOO MANY? ....................................... 36
**PREPARATION** ....................................................................... 39
    PREPARATION AND STORAGE TIPS .......................................... 39
    KITCHEN EQUIPMENT LIST ...................................................... 39
    PREPARATION TIPS .................................................................. 39

| | |
|---|---|
| BAKING TIPS | 40 |
| DECORATING DOG BISCUITS AND COOKIES | 41 |
| DECORATING SHAPES AND CUTTERS | 41 |
| BENEFITS OF DEHYDRATED DOG TREATS | 42 |
| DETERMINING THE CORRECT SIZE TREAT | 44 |
| STORAGE TIPS | 44 |
| HANDLING DOG FOOD – A FEW GENERAL TIPS | 47 |

## SAFETY FIRST — BAD INGREDIENTS FOR DOGS ........................ 49

## GOOD TREAT INGREDIENTS .............................................................. 56

| | |
|---|---|
| MORE SAFE INGREDIENTS FOR HOMEMADE DOG TREATS | 59 |

## CHRISTMAS & HOLIDAY HOMEMADE DOG SNACKS ...................... 61

| | |
|---|---|
| JINGLE BELLS HOLIDAY COOKIES | 63 |
| PEANUT BUTTER CHRISTMAS COOKIES | 64 |
| BANANA CINNAMON CHRISTMAS CAKE | 65 |
| HOLIDAY MERINGUE COOKIES FOR DOGS | 66 |
| SWEET CINNAMON CHRISTMAS COOKIES | 67 |
| BEEFY HOLIDAY BISCUITS | 68 |
| YOGURT-DIPPED GINGERBREAD DOG COOKIES | 70 |
| CINNAMON APPLE CHRISTMAS CAKE | 72 |
| CAROB-DIPPED CHRISTMAS COOKIES | 73 |
| CAROB-DIPPED GINGERBREAD MEN | 75 |
| YOGURT-DIPPED CHRISTMAS COOKIES | 76 |
| CHRISTMAS CHICKEN BISCUITS | 78 |
| NO COOK DOGGIE TRUFFLES GALORE | 79 |
| PEANUT BUTTER MERINGUE COOKIES | 81 |

## CANINE COOKIES & PUPCAKES .......................................................... 85

| | |
|---|---|
| DELICIOUS CARROT CAKE PUPCAKES | 87 |
| SUPER SPICED PUMPKIN PUPCAKES | 88 |
| DOGGIE DROOLIN' PEANUT BUTTER PUPCAKES | 90 |
| QUICK AND EASY CHEWY CHICKEN COOKIES | 91 |
| GOOD SCENT CINNAMON APPLE COOKIES | 92 |
| FROSTING RECIPES FOR PUPCAKES | 93 |

## FUN DOGGIE BISCUITS ....................................................................... 97

| | |
|---|---|
| ALMOND BUTTER CAROB CHIP BISCUITS | 99 |
| CAROB-CHIP BISCUITS | 101 |
| PEANUT BUTTER CAROB BISCUITS | 102 |

## 50 Dog Snack Recipes

SOFT AND CHEWY BEEF BISCUITS ............................................................. 104
PEANUT BUTTER FLAXSEED BISCUITS ....................................................... 105
PEANUT BUTTER AND OATS BISCUITS ...................................................... 106
FLAXSEED BISCUITS ................................................................................. 108
YOGURT-DIPPED PEANUT BUTTER BISCUITS ............................................ 110

**EXTRA SPECIAL DOG TREATS .................................................................. 113**

GINGERBREAD DOG TREATS .................................................................. 115
CAROB-DIPPED PUMPKIN TREATS ......................................................... 116
GLUTEN-FREE CAROB TREATS ............................................................... 118
CANDIED YAM TREATS .......................................................................... 119
NO COOK PEANUT BUTTER YOGURT TREATS ......................................... 120
BACON-FLAVORED DOG TREATS ........................................................... 122
SWEET POTATO SOFTIES ....................................................................... 123
FROZEN YOGURT TREATS ...................................................................... 124
TASTY TUNA TREATS ............................................................................. 125
SUPER SIMPLE BEEF JERKY DOG TREATS ............................................... 126
NO-BAKE CAROB-DIPPED YOGURT TREATS ........................................... 127
GLUTEN-FREE PEANUT BUTTER CAROB TREATS .................................... 128
TURKEY JERKY DOG TREATS .................................................................. 130
NO COOK EASY PB & C YOGURT TREATS ............................................... 131
CAROB-DIPPED FROZEN PEANUT BUTTER TREATS ................................ 132

**DOGGIE BITES AND STICKS ..................................................................... 135**

SPICED BUTTERNUT SQUASH STICKS ..................................................... 137
PUMPKIN PEANUT BUTTER BITES .......................................................... 138
SWEET POTATO STICKS ......................................................................... 139
PARMESAN ASIAGO CHEESE BITES ........................................................ 140
CANDIED BEET BITES ............................................................................. 142
CHICKEN CHEDDAR BISCUIT BITES ........................................................ 143
CHEDDAR PARMESAN BITES .................................................................. 144
BACON CHEDDAR BISCUIT BITES ........................................................... 145
CHEESY CHEDDAR BITES ........................................................................ 146

**ALTERNATIVE TREATS AND INGREDIENTS ............................................... 149**

ADDITIONAL HEALTHY TREAT IDEAS ...................................................... 151
ALLERGIES AND SPECIAL DIETARY NEEDS .............................................. 153
BASIC HYPOALLERGENIC DOG TREAT RECIPE ........................................ 157

**CONCLUSION ........................................................................................... 159**

**ENJOYED THIS BOOK? ............................................................................. 161**

| | |
|---|---|
| **ABOUT THE AUTHOR** | 163 |
| **ABOUT A LIFE WITH DOGS** | 163 |
| **MORE BOOKS BY THE AUTHOR** | 165 |
| **EXCERPT: BONDING WITH YOUR RESCUE DOG** | 167 |
| **DISCLAIMER** | 173 |
| **APPENDIX A - WHEAT-FREE RECIPES** | 175 |
| **APPENDIX B — BONE BROTH RECIPE** | 177 |
| Good and Simple Bone Broth | 177 |
| **NOTES** | 179 |
| **INDEX** | 183 |

## Introduction

I don't know about you, but my family has a long tradition of giving gifts to the pets and having the pets give gifts. My dad always had three special gifts of perfume that he would have their pets give my mom. The dogs always gave the bottle of Shalimar. Within the gift-wrapped boxes of the cats, lay the small bottles of Mitsouko and Guerlain. Every year those gifts for my mom were under the tree, and every year the dogs and cats would receive their special Christmas treats. So it shouldn't be any surprise to discover that I happily wrap gifts for my dogs.

Preparing treat jars full of goodies is one of the fun activities of the season. Let's face it; dogs clearly eat as well as the rest of us. The smells of cinnamon and apple and peanut butter float through my house and cause a tremendous amount of sniffing and nudging when I'm in the kitchen.

**A Word of Caution**

You know your dog's history, his illnesses, and his potential for obesity, diabetes, and allergies. Please keep that in mind as you read through the recipes and make substitutions as needed.

## Holiday Gift Ideas Using Treat Jars

Today the pet industry has become big business and gifts abound for dogs and dog lovers. Still, it says something when you give a gift that comes from your own heart and hands. That's one reason why I enjoy filling those treat jars with plenty of cookies, biscuits and treats.

You don't have to go to a lot of trouble, either. You can use strips of red curling ribbon and baggies or you can pick up a mason jar, fill it with delicious treats, and smack a big red bow on the top. Or, you can invest a bit more of yourself and of your time and create a treat jar that is unique, fun, and even personalized. It's all up to you.

## DIY Treat Jar Lids

Here's a special fun gift idea that doesn't take up too much time and would be appreciated by any dog lover. The idea is to decorate the jar lid. You glam it up with glitter for that fancy French poodle your best friend owns, or you can let your imagination run wild and find fun ways to decorate the lid that conveys a bit about the dog and the dog owner. Sometimes I like to paint the lid and find fun items to glue on top like shells, buttons, or even an image of the dog.

You'll want a glass jar, empty and washed, some glitter, a bit of ribbon, and a gift tag. For the glue, use Modge Podge. A sponge brush is good to have on hand, too.

I like to cover my work surface so I don't make too much of a mess. Use the Modge Podge on the top and sides of the lid and then place the glitter or whatever you plan on using on the lid top. Cover it completely and let it dry for a good ten to fifteen minutes. If you're using glitter, you'll want to do a final coating of Modge Podge to seal. Once dry, a bow, ribbon, and a gift tag are all you need to finish off the jar.

The fun part is making the treats. You can create a mixture or focus on one type of treat. Of course, the real gift is in the treats.

## Fun DIY Treat Bags

While you can make your own bags, I go the paid route and look for simple cotton bags. My Shih Tzu, Teddy, is a bit of a fashionista and often sits on a cheetah print pillow, so when I found some spotted leopard print bags, I knew those would be perfect for Teddy's treats. (Try PaperMart.com.) Once again, you simply add the ribbon, bow, and gift tag and you're done.

## Quick DIY Dog Collar Treat Jar

A quick and easy way to do a treat jar is to make use of a fun dog collar that will easily fit around the neck of your jar (make sure that the collar will fit snugly even with the lid on the jar). You'll also need a type of super glue, a small rawhide bone, and some spray paint that will go with your collar. Maybe match the color.

The dog bone will be the lid decoration, so you're going to spray paint the bone and let it dry. Then glue it to the jar's top. Allow the glue to seal for however long the manufacturer recommends.

Finally, you'll want to create a label for the jar. You can get chalkboard labels from a craft store or even on Amazon and some packages come with a chalk marker. These labels are waterproof and durable. Place one on the front of the jar and write the dog's name, "Woof," or whatever you want. Fill the jar with your homemade treats and you're done.

## Super Easy DYI Dog Treat Jar

You can't get much simpler than this one. All you need is a plastic toy dog that will serve as the lid's top, a washed and clean mason jar easily found at the grocery store, spray paint, duck tape and, of course, a super type glue.(While this is quick to make, be sure and allow a good day or two for the drying time.)

Because you don't want any of the spray paint to get inside the jar (to avoid food contamination), you'll want to thoroughly tape the inside of the lid. Position the plastic dog and glue to the top of the lid. You'll probably need to hold it in place for about fifteen seconds. Then you'll be ready for the spray paint. You may want to go outside to do this part. Spray several layers of pain, allowing each layer to dry for two or three minutes. Once it looks the way you want, allow the lid to dry for one to two days. You'll want to be sure the lid is finished and completely dry before you place your homemade treat gifts inside the jar.

If creating a DIY dog treat jar or bag isn't your thing, don't worry. There are so many places now where you can buy dog or puppy themed gift bags. Of course, you can always go with the brown bag approach, too. No matter which way you choose to package your homemade dog snacks, they will be appreciated with much tail wagging and snout sniffing.

## Holiday Gift Ideas Using Wreaths

Today you can find many examples of fun dog bone wreaths, usually made with commercial dog bones like Milk Bones, on the Internet. You can also create them using homemade dog bone biscuits, so your dogs can enjoy the wreath, too.

Many DIY wreath directions call for a cardboard ring that is smaller in width than the length of the dog biscuit so the dog bone sticks out over the edge. The easiest type wreath to make is when you use a green wreath that is already made

You can use the wreath idea for more special occasions than Christmas. Think of a birthday wreath full of bone biscuits for your dog as an extra special treat. Seasonal wreaths would be fun, too. Be creative and have fun.

TIP: For a forever-non-edible wreath, use rawhide bones.

*Vikk Simmons*

## DIY Easy Dog Biscuit Christmas Wreath

Looking for a quick wreath that you can put up without any real work? This is the project for you.

### Materials

Christmas ribbon of your choosing
Homemade dog treats
Green wreath
Christmas lights, battery operated (optional)

### Directions

If you're going to do the lights, add them to the wreath first. Then glue the battery pack to the wreath. Make sure you have the side with the removable cover face up for easy access.

Space out the bones on the wreath so you know where you want them. Then use the ribbon to attach the bones to the wreath. With these type wreaths, you don't need to use any glue. From the back of the wreath through the built-in wire, pull the ribbon through and cross over the bones to thread the ribbon so you secure all the bones. Wrap the bones tightly so they are secure.

After securing all the bones with the ribbon, you should be at the first bone. Take the two ends of the ribbon around the battery pack on the back of the wreath so it remains secure.

You can take some more ribbon and add a cool big bow at the top and you're done.

## DIY Homemade Dog Bone Wreath

This is a fun easy-to-do project that takes roughly thirty minutes to complete. Your dog will absolutely love having this wreath made of edible homemade dog biscuits.

### Materials

Homemade large dog biscuits (usually 15 - 20)
Scissors and Tape
Cutting Mat and Cardboard
Box cutter
2 Bowls (small and large)

### Directions

Once the cutting mat is in position, place the cardboard onto the mat. Take the large bowl and place it on the cardboard as a guide to use the box cutter and cut a circle.

Once you have the round cardboard, place the small bowl in the center of the circle and cut around the bowl to create a ring.

Using tape, attach the larger ribbon to the back of the wreath. Wrap the ribbon all around the ring until it is completely covered and tape down the end when finished. Space the ribbon as close as you want or as far apart.

Now use the second, thinner ribbon and tie it around the ring, then tape the top securely. Since the ribbon will hold the bone biscuits in place, you want it as secure as possible.

Place the first bone biscuit on the wreath and wrap it with the thin ribbon. Pull tight so it holds in place as you position and wrap the next bone. Make adjustments to the position of the bone biscuits as you go along, always keeping the ribbon tight.

When you get to the end of the wreath, make sure the biscuits are secure and tape the ribbon end in place.

You can use the thin ribbon to create a ribbon hanger and use the first larger ribbon to finish with a big bow.

*Vikk Simmons*

# Beware of Hidden Holiday Dangers

While festive and fun, the holidays can be a dangerous time for your beloved canine companions. There are a number of plants and foods that you may not realize could do real damage to your dog. It's good to take note and pass on the information to your family and friends, too, so they don't accidently give your precious pet something that actually poisons your dog. Also, be careful of leaving food about. You know your dog will find it.

**Poinsettias, Mistletoe, and Holly**

As much as we love to decorate the halls with these gorgeous plants, they can be deadly to your dog. Make sure they are placed high enough so that your dog won't investigate and begin nibbling away at the plants. They are all toxic to dogs.

**Christmas Cake, Mince Pies, and Christmas Pudding**

Mince pies have been a tradition in my family for generations. For many families, these are traditional desserts, but they are a very dangerous food for your dog to eat. They are full of raisins and grapes are bad for dogs. Even one or two grapes can cause a dog to become ill. These cakes and desserts are full of raisins so it's best to keep them out of your dog's reach. In addition to all the raisins, most of these desserts contain alcohol and a lot of fat and suet. Dogs can suffer severe stomach problems and vomiting, all of which can lead to a serious illness.

## Chocolate decorations, chocolate coins

This time of year, chocolate is king. It's not uncommon to find a lot of chocolate coins and these are definitely not appropriate treats for dogs. Make sure all chocolate is kept away from your dog.

## Macadamia nuts and Walnuts

I don't know about you, but I love Macadamia nuts but I have to keep them far away from the dogs. If a dog eats these nuts, he can suffer from vomiting, tremors, weakness, depress, and hyperthermia and be extremely sick for a good day or two. If you think you're dog has eaten any, call your vet right away.

One walnut or a bit of a crushed walnut isn't a problem; however, if black walnuts usually found in Northeastern U.S. and Canada are toxic to dogs. If your dog is busy eating a lot of old walnuts that have fallen from a tree, then he or she may begin to exhibit tremors and seizures. Too many walnuts can also cause stomach problems. Better safe than sorry, so call the vet.

All nuts are high in fat, so it's never a good idea to let your dog eat a lot of nuts, whether they are peanuts, cashews, or any other type. Almond and peanut butter are, as long as they are don't contain any sugar substitutes like xylitol which is toxic and can be fatal, fine to add in recipes. It is always good to remember that moderation should be your guiding light when feeding your dog.

## Bones

For many families, the holiday tables are laden with big turkeys and grand hams. The dogs smell the wonderful food, and it's tempting to throw them a bone but don't. You'll also have to be careful of how you dispose of the bones, too. I don't know about your dog, but mine can ferret through the trash easily enough so I have to make sure I carry the bones out of the house to make sure my dogs stay safe. You may think that the bones from birds such as turkey, goose, or chicken might be safe but they are not. They are hollow boned so they'll splinter and really cause a problem for your dog.

## Alcohol

Not only are there plenty of parties and family gatherings but the use of alcohol increases during the holidays because of its use in many recipes. No rum balls for the dogs, or any other food that has a bit of alcohol.

## What You Can Do

If you suspect that your dog has consumed any of the above items, contact your vet or a local veterinary clinic immediately. Don't wait. You may or may not know how much of the food has been eaten but if you can figure it out, that's helpful. Also, with chocolate, it's helpful to know what type of chocolate your pet may have consumed. There are different grades from milk chocolate to dark chocolate to Baker's chocolate. All cause different levels of reaction.

These are the most immediate food dangers that your dog may encounter a more detailed list can be found in the Making Homemade Dog Snacks section. Be sure and check it out.

## Tips to Keep Your Dog Safe During the Holidays

It's so tempting to have our dogs by our side all the time as we get ready for Christmas or get busy with holiday preparations, but those are the moments when our dogs can come into harm's way.

Don't leave alcohol or coffee within your dog's reach. Pick up the glasses and mugs.

Don't fall into the habit of offering bits of food to your dog as you cook, prepare meals, or put food out. Too much food is as bad for the dog as it is for you.

Prevent accidents and unintended consequences: Keep your dog out of busy kitchens.

Limit your dog's amount of food and treats by having a no-treat rule, and be sure and let your family and friends know.

Don't leave garbage within easy reach of your dog. I find it works best if I immediately take leftovers and the turkey carcass out of the kitchen and in a bag in the garage.

## Making Homemade Dog Snacks

Making your own homemade dog treats for your furry companion is a wonderful way for you and your family to bond with your dog. It's also a good way of making sure you know exactly what goes into your dog's diet – no nasty additives, or crazy amounts of sugars that will have Rover bouncing off the walls for hours on end, or even ultimately harm your pet over time.

There are so many different types of dog treats that you can make yourself that are nutritious and delicious and make for wonderful training bribes.

Making homemade dog treats is a safe way of treating dogs with special dietary requirements, whether they are a new puppy, athletic, diabetic, overweight, and wheat-intolerant or a senior with specific needs. You'll never realize how much better your dog treats are for your pet until you make them. Once you've whipped up a batch of treats yourself, do compare the ingredients to the shop-bought treats. You won't want to go back.

Why is a homemade treat that much better for your dog? Have you ever read through all the ingredients in store bought treats? Do you even have the slightest idea what you're feeding your family pet? You won't have to worry once you use the dog treat recipes that follow. You know every ingredient that goes into your dog's belly.

You might be surprised to learn that homemade dog treats are much cheaper than the overpriced store-bought stuff. Go ahead. Try the recipes. You'll be delighted at how much money you can save – while still spoiling your best buddy.

The do-it-yourself process of making dog treats is pretty simple. Create a list of the ingredients you're going to need and pick them up next time you're at the grocery store. I like to have the pantry stocked so I can bake a batch of biscuits any time one of the dogs gives me that *look*. (You know the one, the pouty hang-dog look.) A well-stocked pantry allows me the freedom to try the recipes whenever I want. In chapter 4, I've included a handy list of ingredients to add to your shopping list.

Many recipes in this collection are quick and easy, while others need a half hour or so to bake. You'll love the Christmas Holiday recipes. Be sure you review all the preparation and storage tips. They will help you save time and ensure that you keep enough tasty tidbits on hand for several weeks at a time.

Is your dog gluten or wheat intolerant? Does your dog have allergies? What about obesity? Our dogs are as prone to this disease as we are. All of this is covered in the additional healthy treat ideas and the allergies and special dietary needs section. You'll find a quick list of wheat flour substitutes as well as the standard substitutions and a basic hypoallergenic dog treat recipe.

What's my favorite part of this entire homemade dog treat thing? My dogs. I love to see those eager, loving faces, and drooling mouths that greet me at treat time. Once you start making your own homemade dog treats, you may never buy store-bought treats again. Let's face it: Not only are homemade treats delicious and nutritious; they are full of love.

**Additional Notes**

Use this section to make additional notes.

*Vikk Simmons*

## Three Golden Rules for Making Homemade Dog Treats

Don't be nervous about cooking and baking for your dog. It's easy if you follow these three golden rules:

### Keep it simple (KISS Method)

Yes, that KISS method pops up everywhere in life, even in the world of do-it-yourself dog treats. Your best bet is to keep it simple. Start small. Don't get overwhelmed. Don't go crazy buying all sorts of ingredients. Take your time, and pretty soon your refrigerator and freezer will be full of all sorts of wonderful, tasty dog treats.

### Only use ingredients your dog likes

It seems like that's an obvious choice, but it's easy to get off track. We can get captured by the super-complicated recipes that call out to us. In our eagerness to great a brand new biscuit or fancy treat, we forget that our dog doesn't like pumpkin or apple or maybe even peanut butter. Make sure your dog likes everything that is in the recipe before you commit to the process.

### Monitor your dog's response and reactions

Maybe you already know that your dog has allergies because he's constantly going after an itch on his paws or a recurring hot spot. If so, make the needed ingredient substitutions. If you're using an ingredient new to your dog, see how he responds. Does he like it? Does he have any reactions? If he loves it, make a note of that favorite treat and ingredient.

## The Health Benefits of Homemade Dog Treats

Homemade dog treats are ideal training aids. Treats are enticing rewards for dogs when they obey commands. However, we do need to be careful when we choose training treats. Even these tiny treats can have a negative effect on a pet's health. Many FDA-approved ingredients may still be harmful to dogs. That's why it's important to check the ingredients of all training treats. The best way to make sure that your dog is eating safe ingredients is to make your own training treats. Be sure and read through the third chapter's list of harmful and poisonous ingredients. Next time you do a little training with your dog, give him a homemade one. You'll find an entire section on training treats.

From quick and easy biscuits to full-on pupcakes, iced cookies, and other delightful treats, there are a multitude of treats you can make for your beloved canines that will help them have a long life full of good health and vigor. With 43 recipes, you'll have your pick of homemade dog treats for that next doggie celebration whether it's a birthday or an anniversary of the day they pawed their way into your heart and home.

## How Many Treats Is Too Many?

Treats are just that, treats. They are not meant to be your dog's primary food source. Too many treats can lead to obesity. Too much weight can lead to heart, joint, and other health problems. In addition, treats should be used as training rewards. Don't give a dog a treat for bad behavior.

## 50 Dog Snack Recipes

Consider the size of your dog when determining the number of calories per day for your dog. Couch-potato dogs should not have a lot of treats. Your dog should only have 10% of his calories coming from treats. If you're not sure, ask your vet how many treats are best for your particular dog. Here is a good rule of thumb for medium-sized treats.

| | |
|---|---|
| Dogs 5 to 10 lbs | 1/2 treat per day |
| 11 to 20 lbs | 1 treat per day |
| 21 to 40 lbs | 2 treats per day |
| Over 40 lbs | 3 treats per day |

If I haven't given any treats as training, I will usually give my dogs a goodnight treat at bedtime after their final bedtime potty run. They know when I say "bedtime treat," that it's time to settle down and go to sleep. We are in for the night.

*50 Dog Snack Recipes*

# Preparation

## Preparation and Storage Tips

Before you embark on making your own dog treats, take a look at these tried and tested preparation and storage tips. They will help you to be organized, save money, and most importantly, always have fresh treats on hand for your pet. But first, let's make sure you have the necessary equipment.

## Kitchen Equipment List

Small and large mixing bowls
Spoons
Measuring cups
Rolling pin
Cookie dough scoop
Cookie cutters (bone-shaped)
Non-stick baking trays or sheets
Ice cup trays (optional)
Dehydrator (optional)

## Preparation Tips

If a recipe calls for mixing dough, have all your ingredients ready beforehand. Measure them into small bowls that you can grab easily and toss into the mix.

If a recipe requires a meat broth, have a go at making your own. Many dogs are very sensitive to the onion powder found in a number of brands of broth. Alternatively, look out for either a lower-salt or sodium-free broth that is just as tasty. (Large quantities of salt are not good for dogs.)

Take a list of ingredients with you on your next grocery shopping outing. If you don't write it down, you might forget it. You might like to consider downloading an app for your mobile that allows you to create shopping lists.

**Baking Tips**

If you and your four-legged friend would prefer crunchier biscuits or cookies, turn the oven off once the treats are done and let them cool in the oven for anywhere between two to six hours or more.

Keep in mind the size of your dog, especially their mouth and the condition of their teeth, when making their treats. Smaller dogs will need tiny, more bite-sized biscuits, cookies, and training treats. Have the right sized doggie biscuit cutter on hand.

Make sure you flour the board before you use a rolling pin. You don't want that dough sticking and creating a big mess.

To make the treats look glossy and rather gourmet, you can brush the tops with an egg wash mixture of water and egg whites.

Preheat your oven before you place the treats inside to cook. You want the treats to be evenly placed with plenty of space around them for good air flow. Make sure the baking tray is in the middle of the oven for even heat distribution.

Remember to set a timer if you're baking treats, but don't only rely on the timer. The time needed for treats to finish cooking is dependent on their size and thickness. Hard biscuits take longer; soft biscuits require less time. Smaller biscuits bake faster, too.

For treats packed with an extra power-crunch, remove the cookies and turn off the oven. Wait for the hot oven to lose heat, so it is simply warm. Put the baking tray with the treats back into the oven and leave them overnight. The treats won't burn, and they will have a fantastic crunch.

Start checking the treats approximately 10 minutes before they're ready to make sure that they aren't becoming overly brown – remember that oven temperatures can vary.

**Decorating Dog Biscuits and Cookies**

You can have a lot of fun decorating your dog's biscuits with dog-approved icing. Be careful of using already prepared commercial icing available at the grocery stores as they are typically full of sugar and are not good for your dog.

While you cannot use chocolate, many gourmet dog bakeries use carob powder as a substitute. When you want to use different colors, try beet powder for pink or red; spinach powder for green; and turmeric to achieve a yellow color.

**Decorating Shapes and Cutters**

Do you know that you can buy an appliance that bakes your dog treats? It's called the Bow Wow Bistro Gourmet Dog Treat Maker. It comes with a bone shaped cutter.

Just as you can find a myriad styles and shapes of cookie cutters for your children, dog biscuit and cookie cutters abound. They come in all types of sizes, themes, and shapes. When you choose your cookie cutter, keep your dog's size in mind. You don't want a huge biscuit for a tiny dog.

Today many dog treat cutters are made of tin or plastic. They are inexpensive but you do have to be careful and dry them really well so they don't rust. The more expensive ones made of copper offer a better option but the plastic and silicone will work equally as well if you want to avoid having to deal with the rust problem. If you are going to use the silicone type cutter, be sure you use a soft, pliable dough that will easily mold into the shape.

I enjoy using the paw-shaped cutters when making cookies for my small dogs. You can find cutters in the shape of squirrels, dog houses, fire hydrants, dogs, and cats. There are more and more shapes offered every day.

**Benefits of dehydrated dog treats**

Some of the common complaints with dog treats have to do with mold, bacteria, lack of texture, and even the absence of real flavor. A big concern concerns shelf life. You don't want to overfeed dogs because you're worried that the treats are about to go bad. Dehydrated dog treats have a longer shelf life.

One big plus when you prepare your own treats is the ability to control the type of ingredients. You can make sure that the food your dog eats is free from all the additives found in commercial treats.

How do you make dehydrated dog treats?

The handy oven method

Using the oven is the fastest, easiest way to begin dehydrating dog treats. One easy way to create dehydrated treats is to use your oven. You simply set the oven at a low temperature like 200 degrees and place the items in the oven to bake for several hours. The time will range anywhere from 200 to 300 degrees depending on the ingredients you are dehydrating. Chicken might take about two hours; veggies might take three or more.

A regular oven works fine, but convection ovens move the process along at a much faster rate.

The easy dehydrator method
For most people, using the oven is a practical and efficient way to make their own homemade, dehydrated dog treats. However, you may not want to tie-up your oven for hours at a time. If so, a dehydrator is probably your best method. You still use the oven but instead of leaving the treats in the oven to dry you move them to a dehydrator to finish the drying process.

In general, you'll place the treats in the dehydrator as a single layer and set the dehydrator anywhere from 125 — 175F. You can then continue baking as your previous draft begins the drying process. Drying time will be anywhere from six to eight hours.

Things to remember

Don't be afraid to experiment. Recipes vary so the amount of time it takes to dehydrate will depend on a number of factors. The first time you use a recipe, make sure you test your treats to make sure they have finished baking in the oven and have had enough drying time. Moisture, amount of baking soda or yeast, even the thickness of dough have to be factored into the equation.

The amount of moisture is a major issue when it comes to the length of time it will take to make the dehydrated dog treats. The more you reduce the moisture content of your treats, the longer they will stay on the shelf. Crispy is good.

**Determining the correct size treat**

We all know little dogs have big mouths when it comes to barking, but many breeds have tiny teeth and small mouths. You have to keep that in mind when sizing your treats. You have to watch the level of crunchiness. Some dogs require softer treats. If so, remember that those treats will probably have more moisture and less of a shelf life.

**Storage Tips**

Baked treats can be kept for between 2 to 3 months when stored in an airtight container and placed in a cool, dry area.

Always label the dog treats with the name and date that you baked them.

If treats have a high fat content, it's best to store them in the refrigerator to avoid spoilage.

If you know your dog won't eat the treats right away, or you've made an extra batch to have on hand, freeze them.

**Additional Notes**

Use this section to make additional notes.

## Handling Dog Food – A few general tips

Food borne illnesses like salmonella can stem from the mishandling of pet foods and treats and lead to serious infections in pets and people. Salmonella can be transferred to people handling contaminated foods, so you should always wash your hands properly when dealing with foodstuffs. Here are a few tips to reducing the likelihood of infection from contaminated foods:

Always buy fresh ingredients that are in a good condition. Watch out for signs of damage to packaging like tears or dents.

Wash your hands for at least 20 seconds with soap and hot water before and after handling food and playing with pets.

Wash preparation dishes and utensils with hot water and soap after use.

Keep pets away from preparation and storage areas.

If you're dealing with raw food, keep it frozen until you're ready to use it.

Thaw raw items in the fridge or microwave, and wash work area surfaces and utensils thoroughly.

Finally, you may find making homemade dog treats is such a delightfully addictive activity that you go on to make them for your friend's and your family's dogs. Be sure you seal them appropriately. Use air-tight containers. For a festive look, wrap a few dry treats in colorful cellophane and secure with a ribbon and gift tag. You might include storage and "best before" details on the tag. Make this a family affair.

## Safety First — Bad Ingredients for Dogs

Pets in general are curious by nature – especially when it comes to food. They're also particularly good at begging when we are cooking or eating. As cute as those puppy eyes may be, though, our dogs can't always tolerate our food. Some of our food may even be toxic and deadly to them.

You may be surprised at some of the ingredients on this list. While there are ingredients commonly listed in dog treats that are perfectly fine, some can be toxic at a certain level. You don't want to overfeed your dogs with too many treats that may lead to potential issues.

Be vigilant and don't assume. If you're not sure about an ingredient, double-check to prevent accidental toxic exposure.

Alcohol
Alcohol affects pets very quickly since it is rapidly absorbed into the bloodstream. When dogs ingest alcohol, it can cause detrimental drops in their blood sugar levels, blood pressure as well as temperature. When an animal becomes intoxicated, they can experience respiratory failure and seizures. Two unknown culprits are yeast-containing dough and alcoholic desserts.

Caffeine
Anything that contains caffeine, including tea, coffee, energy drinks, and even dietary pills, should never pass a pet's mouth. Caffeine can affect a pet's stomach, heart, nervous system, and intestines. Negative symptoms to watch out for include muscle twitching, hyperactivity, restlessness, excessive

panting, increased urination, seizures and increased blood pressure and heart rate levels.

## Chocolate

There are several different kinds of chocolate, and each contains various levels of caffeine and substances known as methylxanthines. The rule of thumb is that the darker and richer the chocolate, the higher the toxicity risk. Depending on what type of chocolate and the amount ingested by dogs, they can experience urination, vomiting, heart arrhythmias, hyperactivity, seizures and tremors. Call the local emergency vet clinic as soon as you think your dog has ingested chocolate with the amount and the type of chocolate ingested.

## Fatty Foods

Foods with high fat levels can lead to diarrhea and vomiting. Ingesting fatty meals can also lead to pancreatitis. Certain breeds are more susceptible to bouts of pancreatitis than others including Shetland sheepdogs, miniature schnauzers, and Yorkshire terriers. No matter how cute your dog is when he sits patiently by your side and stares at you while you eat, avoid the temptation to share your fast food leftovers, foods cooked in grease, and junk food.

## Fat Trimmings and Bones

Table scraps often consist of the meat fat and the cooked bones that we've chosen not to eat. Both are extremely dangerous to dogs. Trimmed fat from meat – either cooked or raw – can also cause pancreatitis in dogs. Although it may seem natural to give a dog a bone, you should be wary of the size as bones can easily choke a dog. Cooked bones (and even certain raw ones) can splinter and cause lacerations or obstructions in a dog's digestive tract. Bones remain a contentious issue, and there's room for a whole other book on this one.

Fruit Toxins
Dogs don't necessarily have a toxin detector. If you give a dog a piece of fruit, even if it is highly toxic to dogs, the dog will probably eat it. Don't assume "it's ok, it's only fruit." Take peaches, plums and persimmons – their pits or seeds are a major problem and can cause a dog's small intestine to flare up. They're also a cause of intestinal obstruction. Furthermore, the pits of plums and peaches contain a certain amount of cyanide that is poisonous to both dogs and humans if the pit is broken and ingested. Dogs love apples, but beware of the seeds, core, and stem.

Grapes and raisins are well known to cause acute kidney failure in dogs. When a dog's kidneys fail, he loses the ability to produce urine and is unable to filter the toxins out of his system. To date the amount of grapes or raisins that need to be consumed to cause such problems is unknown. Avoid grapes and raisins altogether.

Dairy Products and Milk
On a hot day, you may be tempted to share a lick of your ice cream with your dog. Stop and think again. Milk, as well as milk-based products, can lead to diarrhea and other digestive issues because adult dogs don't have the lactase necessary to digest milk.

## Mushrooms

Wild mushrooms, typically found growing in the backyard or along nature trails where you walk regularly, contain toxins that can trigger various organ systems like the brain, liver, and kidneys. Nervous system abnormalities include coma, seizure, vomiting and death – all of which could result when a dog eats mushrooms.

## Nutmeg

How many of us keep nutmeg in the pantry along with other possibly hazardous ingredients for pets? Nutmeg is a common ingredient for baking, and the rich, spicy scent of nutmeg is appealing to dogs. High levels of this spice can be fatal, though and signs to look out for include seizures, tremors, and other nervous system abnormalities.

## Nuts

Nuts are abundant in foodstuffs such as candies and cookies, and there are certain nuts that dogs should not consume. Pistachios, almonds and non-moldy walnuts, in particular, can result in upset stomachs or a blockage in the esophagus or intestinal tract. Moldy walnuts and also macadamia nuts can lead to toxic poisonings. Toxic chemical products produced by fungi that result in neurological signs and seizures are found in moldy walnuts. Vomiting, lethargy, and loss of muscle control are a few of the effects from nuts that can happen to your dog.

## Garlic and Onions

**Garlic** in very small quantities acts as a good tick and flea repellent, but you need to tread cautiously. Garlic, leeks, and chives are part of the Allium family which is poisonous to pets. High quantities can lead to oxidative damage to red blood cells and upset stomachs too, including oral irritation, diarrhea, nausea, abdominal pain, and drooling). Other signs of anemia to look out for include weakness, respiratory rate, exercise intolerance, and collapse.

**Onions** contain something called thiosulphate that is highly toxic to dogs. If your dog is fed onions, onion powder or cooked onions, the dog may come down with hemolytic anemia that results in damage to the red blood cells. You won't see the effect right way as this poison often has a delayed onset. Clinical signs may not show up for several days. Don't wait. Seek veterinary care immediately.

Baby Food
Baby food is a common ingredient in homemade treats and is fine in the small amounts suggested in the recipes; however, some brands contain onions or onion powder – be sure to read labels before buying. Commercial baby food may also contain excess sugar and sodium. If your recipe calls for baby food, make sure you purchase the organic variety. Organic baby food will not have the high sugar and sodium levels.

Cheese
Although not poisonous, some dogs are sensitive to dairy products. Some dogs are even lactose intolerant. Use soy milk, almond milk or lactose-free milk as alternatives. If your dog has a sensitive tummy, use lactose-free cheese or cheeses that have an almond or soy base.

## Liver

Liver is a great addition to dog treats, especially training treats – and that aroma is pretty hard to ignore and most dogs will gladly obey for a taste of liver. While not poisonous, large amounts of cooked liver can lead to vitamin A toxicity. Avoid a complete reliance on liver treats. Mix things up with treat tastes, so that you don't overload your dog's system with a single ingredient.

## Potatoes

There isn't a problem with potatoes (sweet potatoes are particularly nutritious for dogs) but the green parts are toxic. In potatoes and other Solanum species like tomatoes, the green part, when eaten in large quantities, can be dangerous. But a little potato here and there shouldn't cause any problems.

## Salt

Many people love salt because it adds so much flavor. Dogs have fewer taste buds than humans. They get their "taste" of food through their amazing sense of smell. Salt is unnecessary. Too much salt can cause kidney disease and pose a risk of sodium ion toxicity.

## Sugars and Sweeteners

For the same reason that salt is avoided, sugars and sweeteners are not needed or missed. Dogs don't need them. In addition, if you make it a practice to constantly feed sugar to your dog, experts say your dog may end up with hypoglycemia, tooth decay, and obesity. Artificial sweeteners are worse as they are poisonous for dogs.

Other potential dangers to avoid

Apple core pips — while the fruit of the apple is a wonderful treat for your dog, the seeds and core are not.

Avocados – persin is the toxic ingredient in avocados. It's unknown whether the poison comes from the bark, leaves, skin, seed or flesh.

Broccoli in large amounts

Corn cobs

Hops

Pear pips

Plum kernels

Potato skins, especially green skins

Rhubarb, leaves are dangerous

Spoiled and moldy foods, particularly prawn heads and fish

Xylitol, a natural substance often used as a sugar substitute is highly toxic to dogs even in small amounts.

## Good Treat Ingredients

Grocery shelves stock a wide range of human-grade, good-for-dogs ingredients perfect for homemade dog treats. Remember, though, that dog treats don't constitute a complete and balanced diet. Always check with your vet before introducing new foods – especially if your dog has weight or other health issues.

If you know anything about Pugs, you know they have the propensity to blow up like balloons if they simply come near food. My Pug, Charlie, was overweight to the tune of six pounds. Now, on a Pug that is a lot of weight. I rationed Charlie's treats already, but my vet said to take him off the treats as they had too much sugar. At the time, I had commercial treats. When I reduced the treats to one a day — a single good night treat — the weight slipped off, and Charlie lost that huge neck ruff he'd been carrying around for the past six months. Now, with the homemade treats, Charlie is able to have a few more treats and still retain his slim, svelte Puggie figure.

Ready to create a quick grocery list? Make sure you include a variety of these items on your homemade treat grocery list.

Bananas
Bananas are a rich food for dogs. They are high in potassium and that is good for blood vessel and muscle function and also for the regulation of the acidity of bodily fluids. Rich in fiber, bananas are a good home remedy when your dog has a bout of diarrhea or constipation. Bananas also contain magnesium that is important for building protein and

transporting energy, as well as pyridoxine or vitamin B6, an aid in metabolizing proteins and regulating blood cell function in order for the blood to carry more oxygen to the muscles and brain. As with humans, the vitamin C in bananas acts as an antioxidant against cell damage. In addition to the banana recipes in this collection, you'll find a frozen banana is a fun treat for dog who likes to chew. The addition of mashed banana enriches your dog's daily food, too.

Sweet Potato

Delicious sweet potatoes are packed full of nutrients like vitamin C and carotenoids, as well as a host of other phytochemicals and antioxidants. They're also rich in fiber, magnesium, and potassium and are a fantastic source of iron, manganese and copper. Boil the potatoes (these skins are safe unless they're turning green), mash them up with some good olive oil or coconut oil and stuff in a treat dispenser to keep pup busy. Stuffed in a treat dispenser and frozen these will keep your pooch occupied for ages.

Flaxseeds

Flax seeds are simply amazing for a dog's coat, bones, skin and brains and are high in lignans and fiber which are beneficial for insulin action. Be sure to grind flaxseeds up before using them as they are better digested that way and add them to any of your dog treats. Alternatively pick up a bottle of flaxseed oil in the health food store and add a teaspoon to your dog's meals.

Yogurt

Natural, plain yogurt is a delicious and healthy treat for dogs. The active cultures called probiotics help to keep bad bacteria at bay. Yogurt can improve the function of your dog's gut and includes calcium, protein, B12, phosphorous, and zinc amongst other good minerals. A dollop of yogurt is a good way to disguise nasty medicines that need to be given to an ill dog and also helps with urinary tract infections. As a tasty treat, freeze a small portion to crumble up for your dog.

Salmon
Salmon is bursting with omega-3 fatty acids – the good oils. They do great things for skin, coats and brains and help to limit inflamed, arthritic joints and other chronic conditions. It's also a good source of protein. Do be careful of salmon from the northern Atlantic though that is known to contain traces of mercury.

Nori
Edible seaweed packs a punch when it comes to vitamins and minerals and helps to regulate the metabolism.

Blueberries
Fresh, frozen or tossed into a treat recipe, blueberries are potent antioxidants.

Rosemary
Rosemary helps to improve immune function and is a powerful anti-inflammatory.

Pet-friendly Fruits
Dogs love fruit as much as we do. Here are some that are good for your furry pal. Remember, though, that fruits have natural sugar. Give fruit in small amounts to keep your dog's

weight down. Many fruits are good for your dogs; but there are some that cannot be given whole. While you may give an entire apple to a horse, you would never do that for a dog. The apple fruit is fine, but the seeds, stems, and leaves are toxic. The same goes for fruit with pits like apricots and plums. The pits are toxic. Make sure you know which part of fruit is okay to give your dog and which is not.

**More Safe Ingredients for Homemade Dog Treats**

>Apples (no seeds, stems, or leaves)
Baking soda
Barley malt
Brewer's yeast
Broth
Canola oil
Canned pumpkin
Canned vegetables
Carrots
Celery
Coconut
Cottage Cheese
Eggs
Green beans
Ground cinnamon
Ground coriander
Oatmeal
Orange extract
Parsley
Peanut butter
Peas
Popcorn

Pineapple
Pumpkin
Pumpkin puree
Rice
Rice syrup
Squash
Wheat germ
Wheat pastry flour

Lean meats such as pork, beef, and chicken

Goat's milk, soy milk, almond milk, coconut milk.

**Additional Notes**

Use this section to make additional notes.

_____

_____

_____

_____

_____

_____

_____

_____

_____

_____

# Christmas & Holiday Homemade Dog Snacks

The next time you're in a baking mood, don't forget your dog. There are plenty of wonderful recipes that you can try to give your pooch some tasty holiday treats. If your tradition is to create a gingerbread house, how about adding on a dog house? There are plenty of recipes for you to go through with simple ingredients that are probably already found in your kitchen.

*Vikk Simmons*

## Jingle Bells Holiday Cookies

*It doesn't need to be the holiday season for your pooch to go barking for this turkey and stuffing treats. The addition of pumpkin only makes them even better.*

### Ingredients
1 tablespoon of dried parsley
1 1/2 cups of whole wheat flour
1 cup warm water
1 cup of plain bread crumbs
4 oz jar of turkey flavored baby food
2 cups of pure pumpkin (not the pie filling)
2 lightly beaten eggs

### Directions — 350°F (150°C) oven, bake for 30 minutes

Preheat the oven.

Whisk the flour, dried parsley, and breadcrumbs together in a bowl.

In a separate bowl mix the eggs, pumpkin, warm water, and baby food until well combined.

Create a well in the flour and pour in the wet mixture.

Stir this moist mixture very well.

Line a baking tray and scoop the turkey and stuffing treats with a cookie scooper onto the sheet and bake for half an hour.

Turn the oven off and leave to sit for another half an hour to dry.

Cool before serving.

Tip — these soft cookies are tasty for all dogs and especially great for puppies and seniors. Store in the refrigerator for 2 weeks or freeze for up to 4 months.

## Peanut Butter Christmas Cookies

*Dogs love peanut butter as much as we do. Full of protein, vitamins B and E, and heart-healthy fats, peanut butter brings joy to your pooch's heart. I've found peanut butter to be a good motivator, too, so these canine cookies will become a real favorite for holiday treats.*

### Ingredients
2 cups whole-wheat flour
3 teaspoons baking powder
1 cup plain Greek yogurt
1 cup all-natural peanut butter

### Directions — 375°F (190°C) oven, bake for 15-20 minutes

Preheat the oven to 375°F and line a baking sheet with parchment paper.

Combine all of the ingredients in a mixing bowl and stir well until a soft dough forms.

Roll the dough out to about 1/4-inch thick then use a holiday-themed cookie cutter to cut out the treats.

Arrange the treats on the baking sheet and bake for 15 to 20 minutes until firm.

Cool the cookies completely then store in an airtight container and wrap it to give the treats as a gift.

## Banana Cinnamon Christmas Cake

*You're going to want to taste this cake yourself. Talk about smelling up the kitchen with heavenly holiday scents. Make sure you have a Bundt pan on hand.*

### Ingredients

2 cups whole-wheat flour
1/4 cup ground flaxseed
1/2 tablespoon baking powder
1 1/4 teaspoons ground cinnamon
1 cup molasses
1/2 cup canola oil
1/2 cup water
2 large eggs, beaten well
1 1/2 teaspoons non-alcoholic vanilla extract
1 large overripe banana, mashed

### Directions — 350°F (150°C) oven, bake 35-40 minutes

Preheat the oven to 350°F then grease and flour a Bundt pan.

Combine the flour, flaxseed, baking powder and cinnamon in a mixing bowl.

In a separate bowl, whisk together the molasses, oil, water, eggs and vanilla extract.

Whisk the dry ingredients into the wet until smooth and combined then fold in the mashed banana.

Pour the batter into the Bundt pan and bake for 30 to 40 minutes until a knife inserted in the center comes out clean.

Cool the cake completely and cut into slices to serve your dog.

## Holiday Meringue Cookies for Dogs

*Fluffy meringue Christmas cookies were a holiday tradition in our house. Every year my mom baked meringues and filled tins to the brim. Creating meringue cookies for the dogs has an extra-special meaning around our house.*

### Ingredients

6 large egg whites
1 teaspoon cream of tartar
1/4 cup sugar

### Directions — 225°F (107°C) oven, bake for 1 1/2 hours

Preheat the oven to 225°F and line a baking sheet with parchment paper.

Combine the egg whites and cream of tartar in a bowl and beat until stiff peaks form.

Beat in the sugar until smooth then spoon the mixture into a freezer bag and snip off the corner of the bag.

Pipe the meringue mixture onto the prepared baking sheet in the desired shape – feel free to use holiday-inspired shapes like candy canes.

Bake for 1 1/2 hours or until the cookies are firm then cool completely.

Store the cookies in an airtight container and wrap it to give it as a gift.

### Sweet Cinnamon Christmas Cookies

*Who doesn't love the scent of cinnamon? It is certainly one of the main spices linked to the holidays. While cinnamon is not a natural food for dogs, it is a spice that you can use when baking treats for them. Choose the Ceylon Cinnamon made from the Ceylon Cinnamon tree as it has a lower amount of natural occurring courmarin.*

### Ingredients

2 cups whole-wheat flour
3 teaspoons baking powder
1 cup plain Greek yogurt
1 cup all-natural almond butter
2 tablespoons raw honey
1 teaspoon ground cinnamon

### Directions — 375°F (190°C) oven, bake for 15-20 minutes

Preheat the oven to 375°F and line a baking sheet with parchment paper.

Combine all of the ingredients in a mixing bowl and stir well until it forms a soft dough.

Roll the dough out to about 1/4-inch thick then use a holiday-themed cookie cutter to cut out the treats.

Arrange the treats on the baking sheet and bake for 15 to 20 minutes until firm.

Cool the cookies completely then store in an airtight container and wrap it to give the treats as a gift.

**Beefy Holiday Biscuits**

*The way dogs stare and drool at the pot on the stove, you probably assume that beef stock is a perfect food item for dogs. You'd be right. If you want to shower your dog with love, you could make the beef bone broth. Of course, you might want to pull out a drool rag when you do. Bone broth is full of nutrients, especially those that help keep joints healthy. (Hint: great biscuit for elderly dogs.) Check the appendix for the Bone Broth recipe.*

**Ingredients**

1 cup whole-wheat flour
4 tablespoons ground flaxseed
3 1/2 tablespoons brewer's yeast
1 teaspoon salt
1/2 cup beef stock (low-sodium)

1 1/2 tablespoons vegetable oil
1 tablespoon beef tallow
1 large egg white, beaten well

**Directions — 450°F (232°C) oven, bake for 20 minutes**

Preheat the oven to 450°F and line a baking sheet with parchment.

Combine the flour, flaxseed, yeast and salt in a mixing bowl.

In a separate bowl, whisk together the beef stock, vegetable oil and beef tallow.

Whisk in the flour mixture until it forms a dough.

Roll the dough out to about 1/2-inch thickness and use Christmas-themed cookie cutters to cut out the biscuits.

Arrange the biscuits on the baking sheet and bake for 10 minutes.

Brush the biscuits with the egg whites then bake for another 10 minutes.

Turn off the oven and allow the biscuits to cool with the door closed for 1 1/2 to 2 hours.

Cool the treats completely then store in an airtight container and wrap it to give the treats as a gift.

## Yogurt-Dipped Gingerbread Dog Cookies

*This fun recipe combines both ginger and yogurt to make a delightful cookie for your dog. To add a super-healthy edge to the cookie, use blackstrap molasses. It's full of nutrients and has zero fat. If your dog is prone to arthritis, anemia, or diabetes, talk to your vet about the potential benefits and dosage of adding molasses to their diet.*

### Ingredients

3 cups whole-wheat flour
1 1/4 teaspoon ground cinnamon
3/4 teaspoon ground ginger
Pinch ground cloves
1/2 cup water
1/2 cup molasses
1/3 cup canola oil
1 1/2 cups plain yogurt
1/4 cup honey

### Directions — 350°F (150°C) oven, bake for 20 minutes

Preheat the oven to 350°F and line a baking sheet with parchment paper.

Combine the flour, cinnamon, ginger, and cloves in a mixing bowl.

Whisk in the water, molasses and canola oil until it forms a dough.

Roll out the dough to 1/4 inch thick then use a holiday-themed cookie cutter to cut out the biscuits.

Arrange the biscuits on the baking sheet and bake for 20 minutes until browned and very hard.

Place the yogurt in a food processor and add the honey.

Blend the mixture until smooth then brush it onto the cooled cookies or dip them in the mixture.

Place the cookies on a parchment-lined baking sheet and place in the refrigerator until the yogurt dip has hardened.

Store in an airtight container and wrap it to give the treats as a gift.

**Additional Notes**

Use this section to make additional notes.

_____

_____

_____

_____

_____

## Cinnamon Apple Christmas Cake

*Dogs love apples and apples are good for dogs. In fact, they can be considered a super-treat. Around my house, I use sliced and chunked bits of apple hidden in toys, frozen in the summer, and added as toppings to their daily food. Do not use the seeds or stems. Also, stay away from dehydrated apples. As with all things, moderation is the best plan even with super-treats.*

### Ingredients

2 cups whole-wheat flour
1/4 cup ground flaxseed
1/2 tablespoon baking powder
1 1/4 teaspoons ground cinnamon
1 cup molasses
1/2 cup canola oil
1/2 cup water
2 large eggs, beaten well
1 1/2 teaspoons non-alcoholic vanilla extract
1 large ripe apple, cored and chopped

### Directions — 350°F (150°C) oven, bake for 30-40 minutes

Preheat the oven to 350°F then grease and flour a Bundt pan.

Combine the flour, flaxseed, baking powder and cinnamon in a mixing bowl.

In a separate bowl, whisk together the molasses, oil, water, eggs and vanilla extract.

Whisk the dry ingredients into the wet until smooth and combined then fold in the chopped apple.

Pour the batter into the Bundt pan and bake for 30 to 40 minutes until a knife inserted in the center comes out clean.

Cool the cake completely and cut into slices to serve your dog.

**Carob-Dipped Christmas Cookies**

*Many people, like me, enjoy a bite of chocolate now and then, and our dogs are as eager to do the same but they can't have chocolate. Lucky for dogs, carob is an ideal substitute. The carob belongs to the legume family and comes from shrub that has edible pods and seeds. Carob is available in both powder and chip form.*

**Ingredients**

2 cups whole-wheat flour
3 teaspoons baking powder
1 cup plain Greek yogurt
1 cup all-natural almond butter
1 cup carob chips
1/3 cup unsalted butter
1/2 cup honey
1/2 cup skim milk

## Directions — 375°F (190°C) oven, bake for 15-20 minutes

Preheat the oven to 375°F and line a baking sheet with parchment paper.

Combine all of the ingredients in a mixing bowl and stir well until it forms a soft dough.

Roll the dough out to about 1/2-inch thick then use a holiday-themed cookie cutter to cut out the treats.

Arrange the treats on the baking sheet and bake for 15 to 20 minutes until firm.

Cool the cookies completely while you prepare the carob dip.

Whisk together the honey and milk in a small saucepan.

Add the carob chips and butter then heat over medium-low until melted.

Whisk the mixture smooth then dip the cooled cookies in the mixture.

Place the cookies on a parchment-lined baking sheet and place in the refrigerator until the carob dip has hardened.

Store in an airtight container and wrap it to give the treats as a gift.

## Carob-Dipped Gingerbread Men

*The Gingerbread Man is a traditional cookie in many families and now your pet pooch can get in on the tradition with this fun carob-dipped cookie. In addition to cookies, you could also bake extra and roll out the dough to make a gingerbread dog house, too.*

## Ingredients

3 cups whole-wheat flour
1 1/4 teaspoon ground cinnamon
3/4 teaspoon ground ginger
Pinch ground cloves
1/2 cup water
1/2 cup molasses
1/3 cup canola oil
1 cup carob chips
5 to 6 tablespoons unsalted butter
1/2 cup honey
1/2 cup skim milk

## Directions — 350°F (150°C) oven, bake for 20 minutes

Preheat the oven to 350°F and line a baking sheet with parchment paper.

Combine the flour, cinnamon, ginger, and cloves in a mixing bowl.

Whisk in the water, molasses and canola oil until it forms a dough.

Roll out the dough to 1/4 inch thick then use a holiday-themed cookie cutter to cut out the biscuits.

Arrange the biscuits on the baking sheet and bake for 20 minutes until browned and very hard.

Whisk together the honey and milk in a small saucepan.

Add the carob chips and butter then heat over medium-low until melted.

Whisk the mixture smooth then dip the yogurt treats in the mixture.
Place the treats on a parchment-lined baking sheet and place in the refrigerator until the carob dip has hardened.

Store in an airtight container and wrap it to give the treats as a gift.

## Yogurt-Dipped Christmas Cookies

*Yogurt is easily one of the best "people" food for dogs and is a good source of protein and calcium. When you choose the yogurt make sure it does not have any sugar or artificial sweeteners. If you're going to make these for a puppy, choose a fat-free yogurt, one that does not contain any fat substitutes.*

## Ingredients

2 cups whole-wheat flour
3 teaspoons baking powder
1 cup plain Greek yogurt

1 cup all-natural almond butter
3/4 cups plain yogurt
2 tablespoons honey

**Directions — 375°F (150°C) oven, bake for 15-20 minutes**

Preheat the oven to 375°F and line a baking sheet with parchment paper.

Combine all of the ingredients in a mixing bowl and stir well until it forms a soft dough.

Roll the dough out to about 1/4-inch thick then use a holiday-themed cookie cutter to cut out the treats.

Arrange the treats on the baking sheet and bake for 15 to 20 minutes until firm.

Cool the cookies completely while you prepare the carob dip.

Place the yogurt in a food processor and add the honey.

Blend the mixture until smooth then brush it onto the cooled cookies or dip them in the mixture.

Place the cookies on a parchment-lined baking sheet and place in the refrigerator until the yogurt dip has hardened.

Store in an airtight container and wrap it to give the treats as a gift.

## Christmas Chicken Biscuits

*Low sodium chicken stock is handy to have around. If your dog isn't drinking enough water, the chicken broth can stimulate his thirst. Also, the chicken stock can help hydrate your dog if you find him refusing to drink or is sick. These are tasty biscuits full of good ingredients that are easy to decorate for the holidays.*

## Ingredients

1 cup whole-wheat flour
5 tablespoons ground flaxseed
3 tablespoons brewer's yeast
1 teaspoon salt
1/2 cup chicken stock (low-sodium)
1 1/2 tablespoons vegetable oil
1 large egg white, beaten well

## Directions — 450°F (262°C) oven, bake for 20 minutes

Preheat the oven to 450°F and line a baking sheet with parchment.

Combine the flour, flaxseed, yeast and salt in a mixing bowl.

In a separate bowl, whisk together the chicken stock and vegetable oil.

Whisk in the flour mixture until it forms a dough.

Roll the dough out to about 1/2-inch thickness and use Christmas-themed cookie cutters to cut out the biscuits.

Arrange the biscuits on the baking sheet and bake for 10 minutes.

Brush the biscuits with the egg whites then bake for another 10 minutes.

Turn off the oven and allow the biscuits to cool with the door closed for 1 1/2 to 2 hours.

Cool the treats completely then store in an airtight container and wrap it to give the treats as a gift.

**No Cook Doggie Truffles Galore**

*Truffles, even doggie ones, are great for any holiday. It's so much fun to share a bit of "chocolate" with the dogs. You may be wondering whether carob is toxic for dogs. Well, it's not. This is one chocolate-like ingredient you and your dog can enjoy together. An extra nice plus is that you don't have to store these treats in the refrigerator.*

**Ingredients**

1/2 cup peanut butter
1/3 cup whole wheat flour
1/4 teaspoon non-alcoholic vanilla extract
2 cups carob chips

**Directions**

In a medium bowl combine the peanut butter and whole wheat flour.

Add the vanilla and mix well into a moist dough. If the dough is too dry, add a little water a teaspoonful at a time until it is firm but not too sticky.

Roll the dough into 1-inch balls or smaller for a small do and place on a lined cookie sheet.

In a microwavable bowl melt the carob chips on high for 30 seconds and stir.

Microwave in 10-second increments until fully melted.

Use a toothpick to dunk the truffles into the carob and place on the cookie sheet to dry.

Store in an airtight container in a cool, dry place. These delights will stay fresh for a couple of weeks and don't need to be put in the fridge.

**Tip** — *recipe yields between 12 and 15 truffles.*

## Peanut Butter Meringue Cookies

*For a really special holiday or birthday treat, how about a double-packed cookie of peanut butter and meringue? Use caution and common sense with this recipe as it contains sugar. You don't want to overfeed your dog. Offer these as special treats, maybe at bed time. Do not use artificial sugar substitutes, especially Xylitol, as they are bad for dogs.*

### Ingredients

6 large egg whites
1 teaspoon cream of tartar
1/4 cup sugar
2 tablespoons all-natural peanut butter

### Directions — 225°F (107°C) oven, bake for 1 1/2 hours

Preheat the oven to 225°F and line a baking sheet with parchment paper.

Combine the egg whites and cream of tartar in a bowl and beat until stiff peaks form.

Beat in the sugar and peanut butter until smooth.

Spoon the mixture into a freezer bag and snip off the corner of the bag.

Pipe the meringue mixture onto the prepared baking sheet in the desired shape – feel free to use holiday-inspired shapes like candy canes.

Bake for 1 1/2 hours or until the cookies are firm then cool completely.

Store the cookies in an airtight container and wrap it to give it as a gift.

***Additional Notes***

Use this section to make additional notes.

_____

_____

_____

_____

_____

_____

## 50 Dog Snack Recipes

## Canine Cookies & Pupcakes

What dog doesn't enjoy a cookie treat? I know mine do. You'll find their cookies are easily as good to eat as ours. If your dog is wheat intolerant, don't worry. While most recipes are made with wheat, you can always substitute flours. Be sure and check out the flour substitutes in the allergies and special dietary needs section. Meanwhile, head to the kitchen. I'm sure your furry friend will love these mouth-watering recipes.

Remember, you can make homemade dog treats that are appropriate for your dog's size. Regular size muffin tins are perfect for the larger dogs. If you have a small dog, try using mini-cup cake tins. You can even cut those mini-cakes down to an even smaller size.

*Vikk Simmons*

## Delicious Carrot Cake Pupcakes

*You might not think of carrots being good food for dogs, but they are. In fact, baby carrots are great for a dog's teeth. If your dog has put a little weight on, carrots are great low calorie snacks all by themselves. Your dog will love this carrot cake recipe.*

## Ingredients

1 cup whole-wheat flour
1/3 cup old-fashioned oats
1 1/4 teaspoon baking soda
3/4 teaspoon ground cinnamon
1/3 cup all-natural almond butter
1/4 cup canola oil
1/4 cup honey
1 large egg, beaten
1 cup grated carrots

## Directions — 350°F (150°C) oven, bake for 16-22 minutes

Preheat the oven to 350°F and line a muffin tin with paper liners.

Combine the flour, oats, baking soda, and cinnamon in a mixing bowl.

In a separate bowl, whisk together the canola oil, honey, almond butter and egg until well combined.

Stir the dry ingredients into the wet ingredients and fold in the carrots.

Spoon the mixture into the prepared pan, filling the cups about 1/4 full.

Bake for 16 to 22 minutes until a knife inserted in the center comes out clean.

Cool the cupcakes completely before serving them to your dog.

**Super Spiced Pumpkin Pupcakes**

*This recipe will bring home the holiday season with the aroma of cinnamon and pumpkin. Your dog will be thrilled to find a pumpkin treat. In addition to being tasty, pumpkin has a lot of medicinal value for dogs, too. When you're filling your holiday shopping cart, add a few cans of pumpkin as it is good for both constipation and diarrhea. Because pumpkin is loaded with Vitamin A and too much can be toxic, give your puppies a few teaspoons and your adult dogs a few tablespoons.*

**Ingredients**

1 cup whole-wheat flour
1/3 cup old-fashioned oats
1 1/4 teaspoon baking soda
1/2 teaspoon ground cinnamon
1/3 cup pumpkin puree
1/4 cup canola oil
1/4 cup honey
1 large egg, beaten
1 cup grated carrots

## Directions — 350°F (150°C) oven, bake for 16-22 minutes

Preheat the oven to 350°F and line a muffin tin with paper liners.

Combine the flour, oats, baking soda, and cinnamon in a mixing bowl.

In a separate bowl, whisk together the canola oil, honey, pumpkin and egg until well combined.

Stir the dry ingredients into the wet ingredients and fold in the carrots.

Spoon the mixture into the prepared pan, filling the cups about 3/4 full.

Bake for 16 to 22 minutes until a knife inserted in the center comes out clean.

Cool the cupcakes completely before serving them to your dog.

## Doggie Droolin' Peanut Butter Pupcakes

*While peanut butter is a common ingredient in recipes for dogs, remember to check the label and make sure what you buy does NOT contain xylitol. Xylitol is a sugar substitute that is really bad for dogs.*

### Ingredients

1 cup whole-wheat flour
1/3 cup old-fashioned oats
1 1/4 teaspoon baking soda
1/3 cup all-natural peanut butter
1/4 cup canola oil
1/4 cup honey
1 large egg, beaten
1 cup grated carrots

### Directions — 350°F (150°C) oven, bake for 16-22 minutes

Preheat the oven to 350°F and line a muffin tin with paper liners.

Combine the flour, oats and baking soda in a mixing bowl.

In a separate bowl, whisk together the canola oil, honey, peanut butter and egg until well combined.

Stir the dry ingredients into the wet ingredients and fold in the carrots.

Spoon the mixture into the prepared pan, filling the cups about 3/4 full.

Bake for 16 to 22 minutes until a knife inserted in the center comes out clean.

Cool the cupcakes completely then frost with a thin layer of peanut butter.

## Quick and Easy Chewy Chicken Cookies

*You will often find recipes calling for chicken, lamb, or beef baby food, which is fine, but always check the ingredients. You never want to give your dog any food that contains onions or garlic. These are fast treats and great for elderly dogs and those who might have some dental issues.*

### Ingredients

2 (4-ounce) jars chicken baby food
1/4 cup ground flaxseed
1/4 cup powdered dry milk

### Directions — 300°F (148°C) oven, bake for 15 minutes

Preheat the oven to 300°F and line a baking sheet with parchment paper.

Combine the ingredients in a bowl and blend smooth.

Roll the mixture into small balls and place them on the baking sheet.

Flatten the balls with a fork then bake for 15 minutes until browned. Cool completely and store in the refrigerator.

## Good Scent Cinnamon Apple Cookies

*Here's another recipe that will fill your kitchen with traditional holiday scents and make your dog drool in the process. Oats are great for your dog and safe for dogs that have wheat allergies.*

### Ingredients

3 cups old-fashioned oats
1 3/4 cups unsweetened applesauce
1 teaspoon non-alcoholic vanilla extract
1/2 teaspoon ground cinnamon

### Directions — 350°F (150°C) oven, bake for 15 minutes

Preheat the oven to 350°F and line a baking sheet with parchment.

Combine the ingredients in a food processor and blend smooth.

Drop the mixture in heaping spoonfuls onto the baking sheet.

Bake for 15 minutes until browned and firm.

Cool the treats completely then store in an airtight container and wrap it to give the treats as a gift.

## Frosting Recipes for Pupcakes

*It's always fun to decorate dog treats, so here are a few frostings that will delight your pooch. You can also use a simple egg wash, too. Apply the egg wash to the biscuit or cookie ahead of time and then bake.*

Cinnamon Frosting

Combine the following ingredients and mix thoroughly:

1 teaspoon honey
12 oz of nonfat cream cheese
1 teaspoon vanilla
3 teaspoons cinnamon

Carob Frosting

Combine the ingredients below and blend well:

3 teaspoons carob powder
12 oz nonfat cream cheese
1 teaspoon honey
1 teaspoon vanilla

Banana Carob Frosting

Combine the ingredients below and mix well:

1 teaspoon cinnamon
2 cups ripe banana, mashed
3 tablespoon unbleached flour
1 tablespoon butter

2 teaspoons vanilla
6 tablespoon carob powder

Simple Egg Wash

Combine the two ingredients below and use as a wash to decorate your treat *before* you bake. (You don't want to serve your dog raw egg.)

1 egg, beaten
1 teaspoon water

**Additional Notes**

Use this section to make additional notes.

*50 Dog Snack Recipes*

## Fun Doggie Biscuits

Some folks may wonder whether there is any real difference between cookies and biscuits for dogs. Primarily, you'll find the dog biscuit to be hard and often dry. These are usually the ones that come in the shape of dog bones. To make sure your biscuits are hard and crunchy for your furry pal, leave them in the oven at a low temperature for several hours.

*Vikk Simmons*

## Almond Butter Carob Chip Biscuits

*Almond butter is a safe food for dogs as long as it doesn't contain xylitol, chocolate, or any other toxic food. The best choice is probably to go for a natural, plain almond butter and not the type that is flavored. Almond butter has more vitamin E than peanut butter so that's a plus for a healthy coat and skin.*

### Ingredients

2 cups whole-wheat flour
3/4 cups old-fashioned oats
1 tablespoon carob powder
1 cup all-natural almond butter
1 cup skim milk
1/3 cup carob chips

### Directions — 350°F (150°C) oven, bake for 15 minutes

Preheat the oven to 350°F and line a baking sheet with parchment.

Combine the flour, oats and carob powder in a mixing bowl.

Heat the almond butter in the microwave at 10-second intervals until creamy then whisk in the milk.

Stir the almond butter mixture into the dry ingredients until it forms a thick dough then fold in the carob chips.

Pinch off pieces of dough and roll them into 1-inch balls.

Arrange the balls on the baking sheet and flatten them by hand.

Bake for 15 minutes until browned and firm.

Cool the treats completely then store in an airtight container and wrap it to give the treats as a gift.

**Additional Notes**

Use this section to make additional notes.

## Carob-Chip Biscuits

*Your dog will love this biscuits. The carob chips give dogs a safe chocolate chip style biscuit or cookie since dogs cannot have any chocolate at all. You could also substitute plain yogurt chips for the carob, too.*

### Ingredients

3 cups whole-wheat flour
2 1/2 cups bread flour
2 tablespoons honey
1 teaspoon salt
3 large eggs, beaten
1 cup canola oil
1 cup water
1/3 cup powdered milk
1/2 cup mini carob chips

### Directions — 375°F (190°C) oven, bake for 35-45 minutes

Preheat the oven to 375°F and line a baking sheet with parchment paper.

Combine the flours, flaxseed, brown sugar and salt in a mixing bowl.

Stir in the eggs and canola oil until well combined.

Whisk together the water and powdered milk then stir into the mixture until it forms a firm dough.

Cover the dough with a clean towel and let rest for 20 minutes.

Roll out the dough to 1/2-inch thick then use a holiday-themed cookie cutter to cut out the biscuits.

Arrange the biscuits on the baking sheet and bake for 35 to 45 minutes until browned and very hard.

Cool the treats completely then store in an airtight container and wrap it to give the treats as a gift.

**Peanut Butter Carob Biscuits**

*Your dog will love this combination. While milk would not be considered a daily addition to your dog's diet, a little milk in a batch of cookies or biscuits is fine. However, some dogs do not tolerate the lactose found in milk at all. If your dog is sensitive, then you may want to go with something like Esbilac's Powder Milk Replacer.*

### Ingredients

2 cups whole-wheat flour
3/4 cups old-fashioned oats
1 tablespoon carob powder
1 cup all-natural peanut butter
1 cup skim milk

### Directions — 350°F (150°C) oven, bake for 15 minutes

Preheat the oven to 350°F and line a baking sheet with parchment.

Combine the flour, oats and carob powder in a mixing bowl.

Heat the peanut butter in the microwave at 10-second intervals until creamy then whisk in the milk.

Stir the peanut butter mixture into the dry ingredients until it forms a thick dough.

Pinch off pieces of dough and roll them into 1-inch balls.

Arrange the balls on the baking sheet and flatten them by hand.

Bake for 15 minutes until browned and firm.

Cool the treats completely then store in an airtight container and wrap it to give the treats as a gift.

_____

_____

_____

_____

## Soft and Chewy Beef Biscuits

*I love the ease and simplicity of this recipe. Several of my dogs are elderly and actually prefer the softer biscuits, too. Make sure the baby food only contains the meat and does not have onions or garlic. You can also substitute chicken or lamb. I often use lamb for my dogs with more sensitive stomachs.*

## Ingredients

2 (4-ounce) jars beef baby food
1/4 cup ground flaxseed
1/4 cup powdered dry milk

## Directions — 300°F (148°C) oven, bake for 15 minutes

Preheat the oven to 300°F and line a baking sheet with parchment paper.

Combine the ingredients in a bowl and blend smooth.

Roll the mixture into small balls and place them on the baking sheet.

Flatten the balls with a fork then bake for 15 minutes until browned.

Cool the cookies completely and store in the refrigerator.

## Peanut Butter Flaxseed Biscuits

*The flaxseed found in this recipe is a great ingredient for dogs. We all want our dogs to have healthy, beautiful coats and flaxseed can help as it is rich in omega-3 fatty acids. Good for their skin, too. Flaxseed is also a good fiber source, too. I always store mine in the refrigerator in an airtight container.*

### Ingredients — 350°F (150°C) oven, bake for 15 minutes

2 cups whole-wheat flour
3/4 cups old-fashioned oats
2 tablespoons ground flaxseed
1 cup all-natural peanut butter
1 cup skim milk

### Directions

Preheat the oven to 350°F and line a baking sheet with parchment.

Combine the flour, oats and ground flaxseed in a mixing bowl.

Heat the peanut butter in the microwave at 10-second intervals until creamy then whisk in the milk.

Stir the peanut butter mixture into the dry ingredients until it forms a thick dough.

Pinch off pieces of dough and roll them into 1-inch balls.

Arrange the balls on the baking sheet and flatten them by hand.

Bake for 15 minutes until browned and firm.

Cool the treats completely then store in an airtight container and wrap it to give the treats as a gift.

## Peanut Butter and Oats Biscuits

*I find this to be a good old-fashioned recipe for dog biscuits where you can have a lot of fun using the various dog biscuit-shaped cookie cutters. If you haven't looked at the cookie cutters recently, not only can you find dog bones but paws as well as dog houses and hydrants.*

## Ingredients

2 cups whole-wheat flour
1 cup old-fashioned oats
1/2 cup powdered dry milk
1/4 teaspoon salt
1 cup all-natural peanut butter
2 large eggs, beaten well
1/2 cup cold water

## Directions — 300°F (148°C) oven, bake for 40-55 minutes

Preheat the oven to 300°F and line a baking sheet with parchment paper.

Combine the flour, oats, powdered milk, and salt a mixing bowl.

Stir in the peanut butter and eggs until well combined.

Stir in the water about 2 tablespoons at a time until it forms a firm dough.

Roll out the dough to 1/4 inch thick then use a holiday-themed cookie cutter to cut out the biscuits.

Arrange the biscuits on the baking sheet and bake for 40 to 55 minutes until browned and very hard.

Cool the treats completely then store in an airtight container and wrap it to give the treats as a gift.

## Flaxseed Biscuits

*There are a number of types of flour you can use when making biscuits for dogs. In addition to the various wheat flours, you can find rice flour, almond flour, and garbanzo or chick pea flour. Stay away from soy and corn flour as many dogs don't digest those two as easily as the rest.*

## Ingredients

3 cups whole-wheat flour
2 1/2 cups bread flour
1/4 cup ground flaxseed
2 tablespoons brown sugar, packed
1 teaspoon salt
3 large eggs, beaten
1 cup canola oil
1 cup water
1/3 cup powdered milk

## Directions — 375°F (150°C) oven, bake for 20 minutes

Preheat the oven to 375°F and line a baking sheet with parchment paper.

Combine the flours, flaxseed, brown sugar and salt in a mixing bowl.

Stir in the eggs and canola oil until well combined.

Whisk together the water and powdered milk then stir into the mixture until it forms a firm dough.

Cover the dough with a clean towel and let rest for 20 minutes.

Roll out the dough to 1/2-inch thick then use a holiday-themed cookie cutter to cut out the biscuits.

Arrange the biscuits on the baking sheet and bake for 35 to 45 minutes until browned and very hard.

Cool the treats completely then store in an airtight container and wrap it to give the treats as a gift.

**Additional Notes**

Use this section to make additional notes.

_____

_____

_____

_____

_____

_____

_____

_____

**Yogurt-Dipped Peanut Butter Biscuits**

*If your dog is lactose intolerant, then you won't want to use this recipe as it has dry milk and yogurt. If not, then the yogurt is a good ingredient. Choose a plain, nonfat yogurt that does not contain sugar or sugar substitutes (like xylitol).*

## Ingredients

2 cups whole-wheat flour
1 cup old-fashioned oats
1/2 cup powdered dry milk
1/4 teaspoon salt
1 cup all-natural peanut butter
2 large eggs, beaten well
1/2 cup cold water
1 1/2 cups plain yogurt
1/4 cup honey

## Directions — 300°F (148°C) oven, bake for 40-55 minutes

Preheat the oven to 300°F and line a baking sheet with parchment paper.

Combine the flour, oats, powdered milk, and salt a mixing bowl.

Stir in the peanut butter and eggs until well combined.

Stir in the water about 2 tablespoons at a time until it forms a firm dough.

Roll out the dough to 1/4 inch thick then use a holiday-themed cookie cutter to cut out the biscuits.

Arrange the biscuits on the baking sheet and bake for 40 to 55 minutes until browned and very hard.

Place the yogurt in a food processor and add the honey.

Blend the mixture until smooth then brush it onto the cooled cookies.

Place the cookies on a parchment-lined baking sheet and place in the refrigerator until the yogurt dip has hardened.

Store in an airtight container and wrap it to give the treats as a gift.

**Additional Notes**

Use this section to make additional notes.

## Extra Special Dog Treats

Around my house treats reign supreme. However, I do limit the number of treats given each day. Charlie the Pug puts on weight at the mere whiff of a treat. The other dogs would gladly trade their dog food breakfast for a stack of their favorite cookies. While it can be hard to limit their treat and cookie intake when they are staring and drooling, it must be done.

I also make mini-treats that I can keep on hand for training. They come in handy when it's time to reinforce a command or initiate a new behavior. It's always a joy to watch them run outside for the "bedtime potty" and rush to their crates for their bedtime treats. I swear they can all tell time. They know the bedtime hour.

## Gingerbread Dog Treats

*This treat has a wonderful aroma as it contains cinnamon, ginger, and cloves. You know your dog's snout will push and poke to hurry the baking along. Have fun with this recipe and create gingerbread men, dog houses, and bone-shaped treats.*

**Ingredients**

3 cups whole-wheat flour
1 1/4 teaspoon ground cinnamon
3/4 teaspoon ground ginger
Pinch ground cloves
1/2 cup water
1/2 cup molasses
1/3 cup canola oil

**Directions— 350°F (150°C) oven, bake for 20 minutes**

Preheat the oven to 350°F and line a baking sheet with parchment paper.

Combine the flour, cinnamon, ginger, and cloves in a mixing bowl.

Whisk in the water, molasses and canola oil until it forms a dough.

Roll out the dough to 1/4 inch thick then use a holiday-themed cookie cutter to cut out the biscuits.

Arrange the biscuits on the baking sheet and bake for 20 minutes until browned and very hard.

Cool the treats completely then store in an airtight container and wrap it to give the treats as a gift.

## Carob-Dipped Pumpkin Treats

*This is a nice treat recipe if your dog is allergic to wheat. The addition of pumpkin and molasses also makes them healthy as well as tasty. Be sure and use unsalted butter.*

### Ingredients

2 cups brown rice flour
1/2 cup pumpkin puree
1/2 cup all-natural peanut butter
2 tablespoons molasses
1 cup carob chips
1/3 cup unsalted butter
1/2 cup honey
1/2 cup skim milk

### Directions — 325°F (162°C) oven, bake for 10-15 minutes

Preheat the oven to 325°F and line a baking sheet with parchment paper.

Combine the flour, pumpkin, peanut butter, and molasses in a mixing bowl and stir well.

Knead the mixture into a dough then pinch off pieces and roll them into ½-inch balls.

Arrange the treats on the baking sheet and flatten them with a fork.

Bake for 10 to 15 minutes until firm.

Whisk together the honey and milk in a small saucepan.

Add the carob chips and butter then heat over medium-low until melted.

Whisk the mixture smooth then dip the cooled treats in the mixture.

Place the treats on a parchment-lined baking sheet and place in the refrigerator until the carob dip has hardened.

Store in an airtight container and wrap it to give the treats as a gift.

## Gluten-Free Carob Treats

*The rice flour makes this a great treat if your dog is on a gluten-free diet. The small amount of vanilla extract used in this recipe is fine for your dog. We're just giving a small whiff and taste of vanilla here, but don't leave the extract out where your dog can lap it all up. Vanilla extract contains alcohol and alcohol is quite toxic for dogs. Better, is to use the alcohol-free vanilla extract with vegetable glycerin.*

### Ingredients

1 1/2 cups white rice flour
3/4 cup carob powder
1 teaspoon ground cinnamon
1/2 teaspoon salt
1 cup plus 2 tablespoons water
1 1/2 teaspoons vanilla extract (preferably use non-alcoholic variety)

### Instructions — 350°F (150°C) oven, bake for 10-15 minutes

Preheat the oven to 350°F and line a baking sheet with parchment paper.

Combine the flour, carob powder, cinnamon and salt in a mixing bowl.

Stir in the water and vanilla extract until it forms a dough.

Roll the dough out to about 1/4-inch thick then use a holiday-themed cookie cutter to cut out the treats.

Arrange the treats on the baking sheet and bake for 10 to 15 minutes until firm.

Cool the treats completely then store in an airtight container and wrap it to give the treats as a gift.

## Candied Yam Treats

*While you don't want to feed your dog the candied yams your mother or aunt made for Thanksgiving dinner, sweet potatoes or yams are a great food source for dogs and make delicious treats. You'll note there is a small amount of honey used in this recipe. It's also better to use vanilla extract that does not contain any alcohol, although the amounts found here are safe.*

## Ingredients

2 cups water
4 tablespoons honey
3 tablespoons organic orange juice
1/2 teaspoon vanilla extract, non-alcohol
3 large yams, peeled and sliced 1/4-inch thick

## Directions — 250°F (121°C) oven, bake for 3-4 hours

Whisk together the water, honey, orange juice and vanilla extract in a bowl.

Add the yams, tossing to coat, and let soak for 2 to 3 hours.

Preheat the oven to 250°F and line a baking sheet with parchment paper.

Spread the yam slices out on the baking sheet.

Bake for 3 to 4 hours, leaving the oven door slightly ajar, until the slices are dried.

Cool the slices completely then store in an airtight container and wrap it to give the treats as a gift.

## No Cook Peanut Butter Yogurt Treats

*You can't get much easier than this two ingredient recipe. If your dog is lactose intolerant, then you won't want to do this, but otherwise, the yogurt-based recipe will be fine. Again, do not use any peanut butter that has a sugar substitute in it like xylitol as that is toxic to dogs.*

### Ingredients

2 cups plain yogurt
1/2 cup all-natural peanut butter

### Directions

Place the peanut butter in a microwave-safe bowl.

Heat at 10-second intervals until the peanut butter is melted.

Whisk in the yogurt until smooth and well combined.

Line a mini muffin pan with paper liners and pour the mixture into the pan.

Place the muffin pan in the freezer and let the treats freeze solid.

Store the treats in an airtight container and wrap it to give the treats as a gift.

**Additional Notes**

Use this section to make additional notes.

## Bacon-Flavored Dog Treats

*Bacon. We love it. Our dogs love it. Their mouths water and the drooling begins. Bacon-flavored treats make for wonderful training treats as the dogs are highly motivated. You'll also find wheat germ and eggs in this treat, too.*

**Ingredients**

3 cups whole-wheat flour
1 cup wheat germ
1 cup cold water
1 cup bacon fat, melted
2 large eggs

**Directions — 350°F (150°C) oven, bake for 20 minutes**

Preheat the oven to 350°F and line a baking sheet with parchment paper.

Combine all of the ingredients a mixing bowl and stir into a firm dough.

Roll out the dough to 1/2-inch thick then use a holiday-themed cookie cutter to cut out the biscuits.

Arrange the biscuits on the baking sheet and bake for 20 minutes until browned and very hard.

Cool the treats completely then store in an airtight container and wrap it to give the treats as a gift.

## Sweet Potato Softies

*Talk about a quick and delicious treat, that's what you have here with these sweet potato treats. Sweet potato is another food that tickles a dog's palette. Lots of fiber and vitamins make this a highly nutritious treat, too. These are safe, low calorie treats that your dog will love. Simple, healthy, inexpensive, and easy — what more could you need?*

### Ingredients

Sweet potatoes, sliced into thin rounds

### Directions — 325°F (170°C) oven, bake 15 - 20 minutes

Preheat the oven.

Line a cookie sheet with parchment paper.

Place the potato rounds on the cookie tray and bake for 15 – 20 minutes.

**Frozen Yogurt Treats**

*Great treats for summertime special occasions. Bananas have so much going for them when it comes to being a healthy food for humans and for dogs. Most dogs will love these, although I have one dog that turns his nose up at anything that smells of banana.*

**Ingredients**

1/2 cup plain Greek yogurt
1/4 cup all-natural peanut butter
1 medium banana, peeled and sliced
2 teaspoons ground flaxseed
1 to 2 tablespoons skim milk

**Directions**

Combine the yogurt, peanut butter, banana and flaxseed in a food processor.

Blend the mixture until smooth, adding up to 2 tablespoons of milk.

Pour the mixture into a silicone baking mold (ideally one with holiday-themed molds).

Freeze the treats until solid and thaw for 5 to 10 minutes before serving.

## Tasty Tuna Treats

*Another easy recipe with only three ingredients. Fish is a great healthy food for dogs, especially canned tuna or salmon. I like to use these as training treats, too. If your dog is on a gluten-free diet or has other allergies, you can substitute for the wheat flour.*

**Ingredients — 300°F (148°C) oven, bake for 5 minutes**

1 1/2 cups whole-wheat flour
1 (3.5-ounce) can tuna in water
2 large eggs, beaten

**Instructions**

Preheat the oven to 300°F and grease a square baking dish with cooking spray.

Combine the ingredients in a food processor and blend until smooth.

Spread the mixture in the baking dish and bake for 5 minutes or until set.

Cool the tuna treats for 10 to 15 minutes then cut into small squares and store in an airtight container.

## Super Simple Beef Jerky Dog Treats

*No surprise that dogs love these treats, right? Sirloin. I like a good sirloin myself, so I will usually buy two pounds and use half for this recipe. This is a really easy recipe with only one ingredient. I don't know how much easier it can get. Makes for a delicious gift for the dog lovers on your gift list, too, because they can watch those tails wag and mouths drool in anticipation. Good treats for training, too.*

### Ingredients

1 lbs. beef sirloin

### Directions — 180°F (82°C) oven, bake for 3-4 hours

Preheat your oven to 180°F and line a rimmed baking sheet with foil

Slice the beef as thinly as possible then arrange the slices on the baking sheet in a single layer.

Bake for 3 to 4 hours, leaving the oven door slightly ajar, until the slices are dried out.

Cool the jerky completely then store in an airtight container and wrap it to give it as a gift.

## No-Bake Carob-Dipped Yogurt Treats

*These are fun treats to make for your dog. I like to use the small paw-shaped muffin tin for these when I'm making them as gifts. Other than melting the carob chips, there really isn't any baking.*

### Ingredients

2 cups plain yogurt
1/2 cup all-natural peanut butter
1/2 cup carob chips
3 tablespoons unsalted butter
4 tablespoons honey
4 tablespoons skim milk

### Directions

Place the peanut butter in a microwave-safe bowl.

Heat at 10-second intervals until the peanut butter is melted.

Whisk in the yogurt until smooth and well combined.

Line a mini muffin pan with paper liners and pour the mixture into the pan.

Place the muffin pan in the freezer and let the treats freeze solid.

Whisk together the honey and milk in a small saucepan.

Add the carob chips and butter then heat over medium-low until melted.

Whisk the mixture smooth then dip the yogurt treats in the mixture.

Place the treats on a parchment-lined baking sheet and place in the refrigerator until the carob dip has hardened.

Store in an airtight container and wrap it to give the treats as a gift.

**Gluten-Free Peanut Butter Carob Treats**

*Good treat for dogs on a gluten-free diet or have allergies. These have a nice whiff of vanilla extract, too. It's definitely better to use the vanilla extract that is alcohol free as alcohol is toxic for dogs; however, the small amount of vanilla extract used in this recipe is negligible. Still, I prefer to use the non-alcoholic kind and always recommend it.*

### Ingredients

1 1/2 cups white rice flour
3/4 cup carob powder
1/2 teaspoon salt
1 cup plus 2 tablespoons water
1 tablespoon all-natural peanut butter
1 1/2 teaspoons non-alcoholic vanilla extract

**Directions — 350°F (150°C) oven, bake for 10-15 minutes**

Preheat the oven to 350°F and line a baking sheet with parchment paper.

Combine the flour, carob powder, and salt in a mixing bowl.

Stir in the water, peanut butter and vanilla extract until it forms a dough.

Roll the dough out to about 1/4-inch thick then use a holiday-themed cookie cutter to cut out the treats.

Arrange the treats on the baking sheet and bake for 10 to 15 minutes until firm.

Cool the treats completely then store in an airtight container and wrap it to give the treats as a gift.

## Turkey Jerky Dog Treats

*If you're looking for another easy recipe, this is for you. You want to be sure all the fat is trimmed when you prepare these treats. Dogs love jerky and this makes another good training treat.*

### Ingredients

1 lbs. turkey breast, fat trimmed

### Directions — 180°F (82°C) oven, bake for 3-4 hours minutes

Preheat your oven to 180°F and line a rimmed baking sheet with foil

Slice the turkey as thinly as possible then arrange the slices on the baking sheet in a single layer.

Bake for 3 to 4 hours, leaving the oven door slightly ajar, until the slices are dried out.

Cool the jerky completely then store in an airtight container and wrap it to give it as a gift.

## No Cook Easy PB & C Yogurt Treats

*When I want to whip up some treats in a hurry, this is a go-to recipe. Only three ingredients and zero baking time. Great treats to give as gifts, too.*

### Ingredients

2 cups plain nonfat yogurt
1/2 cup all-natural peanut butter
2 tablespoons carob powder

### Directions

Place the peanut butter in a microwave-safe bowl.

Heat at 10-second intervals until the peanut butter is melted.

Whisk in the yogurt and carob powder until smooth and well combined.

Line a mini muffin pan with paper liners and pour the mixture into the pan.

Place the muffin pan in the freezer and let the treats freeze solid.

## Carob-Dipped Frozen Peanut Butter Treats

### Ingredients

1/2 cup plain Greek yogurt
1/4 cup all-natural peanut butter
1 medium banana, peeled and sliced
2 teaspoons ground flaxseed
1 to 2 tablespoons skim milk
1/2 cup carob chips
3 tablespoons unsalted butter
4 tablespoons honey
4 tablespoons skim milk

### Directions

Combine the yogurt, peanut butter, banana and flaxseed in a food processor.

Blend the mixture until smooth, adding up to 2 tablespoons of milk.

Pour the mixture into a silicone baking mold (ideally one with holiday-themed molds).

Freeze the treats until solid while you prepare the dip.

Whisk together the honey and milk in a small saucepan.

Add the carob chips and butter then heat over medium-low until melted.

Whisk the mixture smooth then dip the yogurt treats in the mixture.

Place the treats on a parchment-lined baking sheet and place in the freezer until the carob dip has hardened.

**Additional Notes**

Use this section to make additional notes.

## Doggie Bites and Sticks

A treat jar full of cookie bites and sticks is a great gift. Bite-sized treats are perfect for the moments when you want to do some everyday spot training. You'll find some recipes here that are great for dogs who suffer from allergies, too. Jars of sticks and bite-sized treats are good to keep on hand if your dog is prone to gaining weight, too. You don't have to feed them bone-sized treats to make them happy.

*Vikk Simmons*

## Spiced Butternut Squash Sticks

*If you like to time your treats to the season, then these stick treats are great for fall and winter. You can also substitute zucchini and summer squash. You can eliminate the salt, if you like. I often do. Great for dogs that are on a diet, too.*

### Ingredients

1 medium butternut squash
1 1/2 tablespoons canola oil
Pinch salt

### Directions — 450°F (232°C) oven, bake for 30-45 minutes

Preheat the oven to 450°F and line a baking sheet with parchment.

Cut the squash in half then scoop out the seeds.

Remove the peel and cut the squash into 1/2-inch strips.

Toss the squash sticks with the oil and spread them on the baking sheet in a single layer.

Sprinkle lightly with salt then bake for 30 to 45 minutes, turning the sticks several times, until browned and crisp.

Cool the squash sticks then store in an airtight container – wrap the container to give it as a gift.

## Pumpkin Peanut Butter Bites

*Great for dogs who can't have wheat; this recipe makes wonderful small bites of flavor that your dog will love. Pumpkin is a great ingredient and has a lot of health benefits.*

### Ingredients

2 cups brown rice flour
1/2 cup pumpkin puree
1/2 cup all-natural peanut butter
2 tablespoons honey

### Directions — 325°F (162°C) oven, bake for 10-15 minutes

Preheat the oven to 325°F and line a baking sheet with parchment paper.

Combine all of the ingredients in a mixing bowl and stir well.

Knead the mixture into a dough then pinch off pieces and roll them into 1/2-inch balls.

Arrange the treats on the baking sheet and flatten them with a fork.

Bake for 10 to 15 minutes until firm.

Cool the treats completely then store in an airtight container and wrap it to give the treats as a gift.

## Sweet Potato Sticks

*Sweet potatoes are one of those super foods for dogs as well as people. The price of a sweet potato is usually pretty low, so this is an extremely cost-effective way of having tasty treats on hand for your pooch. I usually eliminate the salt and am happy to give these out as gifts, too.*

## Ingredients

3 large sweet potatoes
1 1/2 tablespoons canola oil
Pinch salt

## Instructions — 450°F (232°C) oven, bake for 30 minutes

Preheat the oven to 450°F and line a baking sheet with parchment.

Peel the sweet potatoes and cut them into 1/2-inch strips.

Toss the sweet potato sticks with the oil and spread them on the baking sheet in a single layer.

Sprinkle lightly with salt then bake for 30 minutes, turning the sticks several times, until browned and crisp.

Cool the sweet potato sticks then store in an airtight container – wrap the container to give it as a gift.

## Parmesan Asiago Cheese Bites

*These are great tasty bites for your dog. The combination of parmesan and asiago is way less fatty than most cheese and the dogs quickly catch the scent.*

### Ingredients

1 1/2 cups whole-wheat flour
1/4 cup powdered dry milk
1 cup grated asiago cheese
1 cup grated parmesan cheese
3 tablespoons canola oil
1/3 to 1/2 cup cold water

### Directions — 350°F (150°C) oven, bake for 30 minutes

Preheat the oven to 350°F and line a baking sheet with parchment paper.

Combine the flour and powdered milk in a mixing bowl then stir in the cheeses and canola oil.

Add the water two tablespoons at a time, stirring until it forms a dough.

Roll out the dough to ½-inch thickness and use a holiday-themed cookie cutter to cut out the treats.

Arrange the treats on the baking sheet and bake for 30 minutes until browned

Cool the treats completely then store in an airtight container and wrap it to give the treats as a gift.

**Additional Notes**

Use this section to make additional notes.

## Candied Beet Bites

*Beets are high in fiber and are a safe food for dogs. I love the red flavor of these treats and find they are fitting for the holiday season. The addition of blackstrap molasses increases the health benefits.*

### Ingredients

2 cups water
3 to 4 tablespoons blackstrap molasses
3 tablespoons organic orange juice
1/2 teaspoon vanilla extract (non-alcoholic)
3 large beets, peeled and sliced ¼-inch thick

### Directions — 250°F (121°C) oven, bake for 3-4 hours

Whisk together the water, honey, orange juice and vanilla extract in a bowl.

Add the beets, tossing to coat, and let soak for 2 to 3 hours.

Preheat the oven to 250°F and line a baking sheet with parchment paper.

Spread the beet slices out on the baking sheet.

Bake for 3 to 4 hours, leaving the oven door slightly ajar, until the slices are dried.

Cool the treats completely then store in an airtight container and wrap it to give the treats as a gift.

## Chicken Cheddar Biscuit Bites

*Another non-wheat recipe that is great for dogs that are wheat intolerant. Chicken is always a tasty treat for dogs. The combination of cheese and chicken make for a special treat for the dogs.*

**Ingredients**

1/2 cup brown rice flour
1/4 cup skim milk
1/2 cup shredded cheddar cheese
1/2 cup cooked chicken breast, shredded

**Directions — 350°F (150°C) oven, bake for 10-15 minutes**

Preheat the oven to 350°F and line a baking sheet with parchment paper.

Combine all of the ingredients in a mixing bowl until well combined.

Drop heaping tablespoons of the mixture onto the baking sheet, spacing them about 2 inches apart.

Bake for 10 to 15 minutes until the edges are browned.

Cool the treats completely then store in an airtight container in the refrigerator and wrap it to give the treats as a gift.

## Cheddar Parmesan Bites

*This is another cheese treat that dogs will love. Making them bite-size makes them great as training treats. Most dogs love cheese. I know mine do. As long as your dog isn't lactose intolerant, these will be great treats to have on hand.*

## Ingredients

1 1/2 cups whole-wheat flour
1/4 cup powdered dry milk
1 1/2 cups shredded cheddar cheese
1/2 cup grated parmesan cheese
3 tablespoons canola oil
1/3 to 1/2 cup cold water

## Directions — 350°F (150°C) oven, bake for 30 minutes

Preheat the oven to 350°F and line a baking sheet with parchment paper.

Combine the flour and powdered milk in a mixing bowl then stir in the cheeses and canola oil.

Add the water two tablespoons at a time, stirring until it forms a dough.

Roll out the dough to 1/2-inch thickness and use a holiday-themed cookie cutter to cut out the treats.

Arrange the treats on the baking sheet and bake for 30 minutes until browned

Cool the treats completely then store in an airtight container and wrap it to give the treats as a gift.

## Bacon Cheddar Biscuit Bites

*Nothing like adding bacon to the mix to whet the appetite of your dogs. They won't be far while you are making these treats. Be prepared for drooling.*

### Ingredients

1/2 cup brown rice flour
1/4 cup skim milk
1/2 cup shredded cheddar cheese
1 to 2 slices cooked bacon, chopped

### Directions — 350°F (150°C) oven, bake for 10-15 minutes

Preheat the oven to 350°F and line a baking sheet with parchment paper.

Combine all of the ingredients in a mixing bowl until well combined.

Drop heaping tablespoons of the mixture onto the baking sheet, spacing them about 2 inches apart.

Bake for 10 to 15 minutes until the edges are browned.

Cool the treats completely then store in an airtight container and wrap it to give the treats as a gift.

## Cheesy Cheddar Bites

*Great treat to make out of ingredients you probably have on hand as most people seem to like cheddar cheese.*

## Ingredients

1 1/2 cups whole-wheat flour
1/4 cup powdered dry milk
2 cups shredded cheddar cheese
3 tablespoons canola oil
1/3 to 1/2 cup cold water

## Instructions — 350°F (150°C) oven, bake for 30 minutes

Preheat the oven to 350°F and line a baking sheet with parchment paper.

Combine the flour and powdered milk in a mixing bowl then stir in the cheese and canola oil.

Add the water two tablespoons at a time, stirring until it forms a dough.

Roll out the dough to 1/2-inch thickness and use a holiday-themed cookie cutter to cut out the treats.

Arrange the treats on the baking sheet and bake for 30 minutes until browned.

Cool the treats completely then store in an airtight container and wrap it to give the treats as a gift.

## Additional Notes

Use this section to make additional notes.

# Alternative Treats and Ingredients

We all know that dogs are mad for treats, and we know how much we love spoiling them. The problem is that many commercial treats are packed full of salt, sugar, and fat. They don't have any nutritional value. A couple of commercial treats a day and your dog is on the road to obesity and health problems.

Just "ask" any dog, and they will "tell" you that a treat is an important part of their day, so it's unrealistic to ban them completely. Instead, check out these healthy and dog-friendly alternatives for homemade, healthy goodies.

*Vikk Simmons*

## Additional Healthy Treat Ideas

Here are some additional healthy alternatives that many dogs love as treats. Do remember that even though they are healthy, they should still be rationed as treats.

Carrots
Dogs love to crunch raw carrots and are happy to eat them raw. You can even freeze raw carrots and give them frozen. In fact, you'll find frozen carrots do wonders for teething pups to soothe gums, as well as giving them something to chew.

Fresh Fruit
For healthy and tasty munchies, a handful of strawberries or blueberries or maybe a mashed up banana is just the trick. Add the fruit to oatmeal for an even bigger boost. Watermelon and apple are also reliable canine favorites but remember to remove all the toxic seeds before feeding.

Plain, non-fat Yogurt
As noted before, yogurt is great for dogs with a weak stomach. Mix it with your dog's normal meal or add their favorite fruits. Your dog will probably eat yogurt as is, too.

Rice and Beef
Want to get those tails wagging while serving a healthy meal or snack? Cooked rice with lean ground beef will make that happen. The good news is that you can make up a big batch and refrigerate. Scoop just enough into your dog's food bowl but make sure you give it a 30-second blast in the microwave

before serving — don't let it get too hot. You'll find this is a good light meal for dogs with upset stomachs.

Frozen Yogurt Pops
Pour yogurt into ice cube trays or cupcake papers and freeze before serving. A fabulous treat on hot days!

Frozen Banana Pots
Mix a carton of plain yogurt with two mashed ripe bananas and pour into ice cube trays to freeze.

Frozen Peanut Butter Pops
Mix a carton of plain yogurt with two ripe bananas and six tbsp of peanut butter before pouring into ice trays and freezing.

Cottage Cheese and Yogurt
Boil a couple of boneless chicken breasts, cube them, and mix with a carton of cream cheese, a carton of plain yogurt, and a few shredded carrots. Add one tsp of olive oil, mix well, and serve.

Macaroni and Cheese
Boil a cup of macaroni and mix with a carton of cottage cheese. Add some cooked liver or boiled chicken for flavor or even mashed up peas or shredded carrots.

## Allergies and special dietary needs

It's not unusual to have a dog that is allergic to wheat or has gluten intolerance. For these dogs, you certainly don't want to use the standard, more common flours like whole wheat. Also, while buckwheat flour and tapioca flour are gluten free, they may contain wheat flour so you wouldn't want to use as substitutes if your dog has certain allergies. Though they are not gluten free, barley, oat, and rye flours are considered good substitutes for some dogs who find them acceptable.

Wheat flour substitutes

Almond flour

Amaranth flour

Brown rice flour

Chickpea flour

Corn flower

Cornmeal

Kamut and spelt flours

Millet flour

Potato flour (even instant potatoes)

Quinoa flour

Rice flour

Sorghum flour

Soy flour

White rice flour

If you're going to use substitute flour for wheat flour in a recipe, check the following accepted standard list of substitutions:

**Additional Notes**

Use this section to make additional notes.

Standard substitutions for wheat flour

1- 3/8 cups barley flour for 1 cup white flour

1 cup corn flour for 1 cup white flour

7/8 cup corn meal for each cup white flour

3/8 cup potato flour for 1 cup of white flour

7/8 cup rice flour for each cup of white flour

1 cup rye meal for 1 cup white flour

1-1/2 cups ground rolled oats or 1 cup oat flour for 1 cup white flour

1 cup whole wheat flour for 1 cup white flour.

1 cup of wheat flour equals

7/8 cup amaranth

7/8 cup garbanzo bean

7/8 cup chickpea (garbanzo)

3/4 cup corn flour

1 cup cornmeal

3/4 cup millet flour

3/4 cup oat flour

5/8 cup potato flour

3/4 cup potato starch

7/8 cup rice flour

3/4 cup soy flour

## Additional Notes

Use this section to make additional notes.

## Basic Hypoallergenic Dog Treat Recipe

*If you have a dog that is allergic to many items like wheat, preservatives, and additives, a basic recipe geared for hypoallergenic dogs is the best place to start. If your dog requires a grain-free treat, use chickpea flour.*

**Ingredients**
3 cups rice flour
1/2 cup milk
1 cup cheddar cheese, grated
1 tbsp olive oil
1/4 cup water*

**Directions — 350°F (180°C) oven, bake for 10 - 15 minutes**

Preheat the oven.

Pour the rice flour and the grated cheese into a large mixing bowl.

Add the olive oil and milk and mix. Slowly add the water to make the dough.

Mix the dough until it slightly sticky.

Roll onto a mat or surface and use dog-shaped cookie cutters to make the treats.

Bake for 10 — 15 minutes, and then cool.

Refrigerate.

Perhaps your puppy has just weaned onto solids, or maybe your adult dog's teeth aren't quite the strength they used to be, or your dog has special dietary requirements, whatever the issue, there are plenty of delicious, homemade healthy treat recipes available.

Homemade treats are cost-effective, natural and with all the love that goes into making them, your dog will be tail-wagging, tongue-licking happy for sure!

**Additional Notes**

Use this section to make additional notes.

## Conclusion

If you enjoyed reading through these fun holiday dog snack recipes, you should be ready to make them for your eager, hungry, ready-to-please dogs. With 50 recipes, you'll have more than enough to keep you busy during the holiday season.

Have fun with the gift ideas. Imagine coming up with various sized treat jars for yourself and your friends. I'm sure your dog-loving friends will appreciate the time and attention you took, and their dogs will love you forever. Try a hydrant shaped cookie cutter to add a bit of whimsy.

Most of all, I hope you've found a new activity you and your family members can share with your dog. The treats make great rewards for our dog and will help your relationship grow in a positive way. One tip: don't give a treat to your dog while he or she is excited. Withhold the treat until your dog sits calmly in front of you.

This works for me every time. As I've mentioned in my other books, Charlie, my Pug, can hardly contain himself, but he has learned that he won't get a beloved treat unless he plants his behind on the floor and stays seated. Sam, my giant Great Pyrenees, saunters up, sits, and waits patiently. Riley stands at the back, quiet and in a sit-stay waiting for his treat. Anytime the dogs are unruly or excited, instead of yelling, I simply grab a treat and hold it in the air. I don't say a word. One by one, behinds hit the floor and eyes lookup. They know. Only the quiet get the treats.

If you enjoyed this book of recipes, you'll find even more recipes in *Easy Homemade Dog Treat Recipes: Fun Homemade Treats for the Busy Pet Lover.* Also, be on the lookout for more books in the near future.

Have you picked up your 27-page FREE Dog Training and Resource Guide? If not, please take advantage of this simple guide.

Be on the lookout for more books in the near future.

Thanks,

*Vikk Simmons*

## Enjoyed this book?

Thank you so much for taking the time to buy and read *Easy Homemade Dog Treat Recipes: Fun Homemade Dog Treats for the Busy Pet Lover.*

Please leave a review and let us know what you liked about this book by going to

http://www.amazon.com/gp/css/order-history.

**amazon reviews**

*then clicking on Orders.*

## About the Author

## About A Life with Dogs

A confirmed dog lover, Vikk Simmons shares her life with seven dogs and two cats. Vikk is the author of the Dog Care and Training Series books, including the popular *Bonding with Your Rescue Dog: Decoding and Influencing Dog Behavior* and *Easy Homemade Dog Treat Recipes: Fun Homemade Dog Treats for the Busy Pet Lover*. She writes books, blogs, and is an avid dog lover. To learn more about her crazy canine pack and all the dogs, check out her blog A Life with Dogs.

http://www.ALifeWithDogs.com

Let's Connect!

http://www.facebook.com/ALifewithDogs

Follow me on Twitter @PackLeader_Vikk

# More Books by the Author

### EASY HOMEMADE DOG TREAT RECIPES

Book 2 in the *Dog Training and Dog Care Series*, *Easy Homemade Dog Treat Recipes - Fun, Homemade Dog Treats for the Busy Pet Lover*, focuses on building that loving relationship with your dog through cooking and having fun, while sharing pet-safe, treats for love and for training with your beloved dog. Great companion book to *50 Dog Treat Snacks*.

No Oven! No Problem! No Cook Dog Treats
Canine Cookies
Doggie Biscuits
Pupcakes
Easy directions
Special Treats for Senior Dogs
Dehydrated Dog Treats
Training Treats
Doggie Biscuits
Special Treats for Hypoallergenic Dogs
Special Treats for Wheat Intolerant Dogs
Special Treats for Problems (fleas, bad breath, etc.)

# Excerpt: Bonding with your Rescue Dog

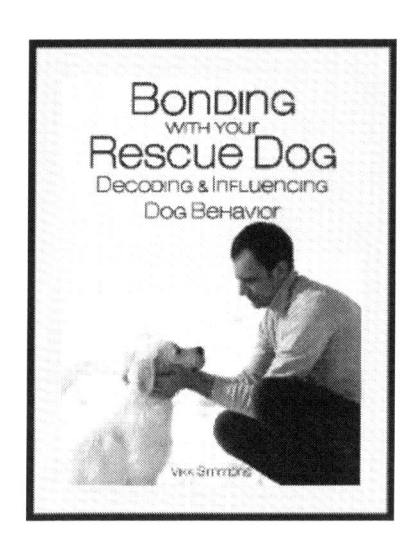

*Two weeks after I was born*, our Asta, the German Shepherd dog who accompanied my dad to Germany and to Korea where he was stationed after World War II, had twelve pups. Decades later, I am still surrounded by dogs.

My first babysitter was a dog. Asta guarded me as I sat in my playpen on the front yard. My first best friend was a dog. As an Army brat without any siblings, our dogs were my earliest and constant companions.

Today my friends and acquaintances often comment on the varied personalities of my dogs and how individual they are. Riley the Cocker Spaniel rock hound is a geologist by trade and loves to bring the best of his river rock finds into the house to decorate his crate. Charlie the Pug can't go an hour without putting on his pouty face about something. Teddy the Shih Tzu and leader of the pack does his best to keep his pack in line but he draws the line with the two cats. Sam, known as the stretch-Cadillac of the Great Pyrenees, demands attention with his noble look, yet all the while he keeps an eye to the sky in search of low-flying planes and helicopters whose appearance sets him off on a gallop leaping into the sky to catch their tails and pull those planes to the ground. There's also a certain amount of fun and pride when walking Sam as we venture down the street, as people seem to think I'm walking a big white horse. Cars slow down, people stare.

Of course Sam is nothing without HoneyBunn the four-pound Mi-Ki who is his ever-present scout watching the sky lanes above. Freddie the Maltese spins and twirls and does his best to garner attention with his dancing bear routine. All are entertained by our newest pack member, Max, the three-year old Great Pyrenees who's become the scourge of neighborhood cats.

Each has made his or her way to my home and into my heart. They are distinct and they are a joy. I am the one who has been rescued.

This book is one small way I can show my gratitude and perhaps help other rescues who are in need of their own forever home.

# Introduction

Science is finally proving what all dog lovers have known for ages. Dogs bring love to their human companions along with some special health benefits. Dogs can provoke a change in mood from sadness to joy in an instant. Feeling their soft nuzzles or stroking them can help lower YOUR blood pressure. Listening to their soft snores can bring calm and a sudden smile. Dogs give back in more ways than you can imagine if you just give them a chance.

Go ahead, if you must. Go ahead and tell me that I'm wrong. I admit that I'm biased: I favor rescues over any other dogs. After all, I currently share my home with a slew of them now. When it comes to the question of where and how to get a dog, I think that, as often as possible, people should go out and adopt a dog that needs a forever home. There are a million all over the world. Yet, when it comes to dog options, as easy as they are, we tend to overlook the importance of deeply understanding the adopted dog's past experiences.

It may come as no surprise to you that it was my very own rescues that inspired me to write *Bonding with Your Rescue Dog*. It would be superficial to suggest that all rescue dogs are similar, but I couldn't believe more strongly that, when you find and adopt that special one that becomes your furry best friend, with all his fears, joy, shyness, devotion and perhaps quirkiness, to understand these canine emotions is to understand dogs. It is definitely motivating.

Understanding your duties and responsibilities is the first step in deciding whether to adopt a dog. All dogs require a large amount of time, space, supervision, love, patience, training, veterinary care, healthy nutrition and exercise. It definitely helps if a dog is chosen with love and with the dog's temperament in mind, and with limited assistance from the brain.

There is no breed that is "best" for you. Many mixed breeds may be nippers or aggressive, or fearful of strangers wearing hats at the dog park. To be honest, selecting your shelter dog is something that just happens, quite like falling in love. Sometimes they simply show up on your doorstep. I met a lovable furry dog outside a bowling alley and he became Jeremiah, my friend and companion, for a number of years. He sat outside the bowling alley's main door for three days and I couldn't take it anymore. No one claimed him, but he had somehow managed to claim me.

Rescue dogs will stretch your hearts and fill them with love and compassion. They will awaken the knowledge that there are so many dogs in shelters and with rescue groups waiting to give you all their love, yearning to be rescued and given a second chance. The hope that you see in a dog's eyes when you visit a shelter or meet your new furry friend through a rescue group, and the lift in your own heart in response, is what adoption is all about.

When you've decided that the time is right and you're ready to adopt your new furry best friend, the best way to determine the right fit for your family is to visit your local shelter or contact a local rescue group. Talk to the people who work at the shelter or with the group. Although a large percentage of rescue dogs are mixed breeds, all dogs, no matter their breed or the mix, are unique and have unique personalities and quirks.

Many future pet parents go online in search of the perfect dog to adopt. There are national registries like Petfinder.com that provide photos and brief histories of the available dogs. That's how I found my beloved Great Pyrenees, Waco the Wonder Dog. The people who are closest to the dogs, such as the workers and volunteers with the shelters and rescue groups, or even the foster parents of the dog, can provide you with some of the dog's unique characteristics.

Every furry rescue will need to be walked, and will have different exercise needs, as well as emotional needs. Before adopting your new best friend, be honest to yourself about your lifestyle. Bring home a dog that has the same energy level that you do. Keep in mind that canine companions are "forever companions," and that this is a lifelong commitment to your dog and to all of his health, medical, nutritional, training and exercise needs and quirks.

Rescue dogs often suffer from anxiety and depression, and will need an adjustment period. Some rescue dogs take longer to adapt, while others fit right in. But what happens when your newly adopted canine companion won't stop barking, is terrified of other dogs and people, growls at your children or won't leave the cats' food alone? Sometimes training an older rescue can be more challenging, but not impossible.

Training our canine companions should never be stressful. Instead it should be fun and inspiring for both you and your dog. The benefits of positive training are huge. Positive training not only strengthens your bond with your dog, but also teaches you empathy, patience and compassion. You'll learn how to understand your dog and what drives him to do the things he does. Training should not be about power and dominance. When using the positive approach, you will start observing some rather interesting behaviors. All dogs are keen to learn. They all want to be praised and rewarded. So forget the old stuff. Punishment doesn't have a place here when training rescues, or any dogs for that matter.

Buy your copy of *BONDING with Your RESCUE DOG* today.
www.amazon.com/dp/B00IGJFJZI

## Disclaimer

© 2015

**All Rights Reserved.** No part of this publication may be reproduced in any form or by any means, including scanning, photocopying, or otherwise without prior written permission of the copyright holder.

**NOTICE** - Readers are urged to seek the advice of their veterinarians before feeding their dogs any homemade food, including the recipes found in this book. These recipes are for treats and snacks and are not meant to replace any dog's normal and regular diet. While most dogs tolerate the food prepared from these recipes, there are dogs that have food allergies and other food intolerances. The author and the publisher cannot be held liable for any resulting problems.

Disclaimer and Terms of Use: The Author and Publisher have strived to be as accurate and complete as possible in the creation of this book, notwithstanding the fact that they do not warrant or represent at any time that the contents within are accurate due to the rapidly changing nature of the Internet. While all attempts have been made to verify information provided in this publication, the Author and Publisher assume no responsibility for errors, omissions, or contrary interpretation of the subject matter herein. Any perceived slights of specific persons, peoples, or organizations are unintentional. In practical advice books, like anything else in life, there are no guarantees of income made or health benefits received. This book is not intended for use as a source of medical, legal, business, accounting or financial advice. All readers are advised to seek services of competent professionals in medical, legal, business, accounting, and finance matters.

Printed in the United States of America

The author cannot be held responsible should any losses, risks, liabilities or damages occur, that may be linked, directly or indirectly, with the information contained within this book.

## APPENDIX A - Wheat-free Recipes

Basic Hypoallergenic Dog Treat Recipe
Additional Healthy Treat Ideas
Bacon Cheddar Biscuit Bites
Candied Yam Treats
Candied Beet Bites
Carob-Dipped Pumpkin Treats
Carob-Dipped Frozen Peanut Butter Treats
Chicken Cheddar Biscuit Bites
Frozen Yogurt Treats
Gluten-Free Carob Treats
Gluten-Free Peanut Butter Carob Treats
Good Scent Cinnamon Apple Cookies
Holiday Meringue Cookies for Dogs
No Cook Easy PB & C Yogurt Treats
No Cook Peanut Butter Yogurt Treats
No-Bake Carob-Dipped Yogurt Treats
Quick and Easy Chewy Chicken Cookies
Peanut Butter Meringue Cookies
Pumpkin Peanut Butter Bites
Soft and Chewy Beef Biscuits
Spiced Butternut Squash Sticks
Super Simple Beef Jerky Dog Treats
Sweet Potato Softies
Sweet Potato Sticks
Tasty Tuna Treats
Turkey Jerky Dog Treats

**Additional Notes**

Use this section to make additional notes.

# APPENDIX B — Bone Broth Recipe

You can't go wrong with a bone broth recipe, and this is a great extra ingredient to put into a homemade treat recipe. Bone broth is so dense with nutrients that it's excellent for all dogs and even more so for the ill or elderly dogs.

Beef bones, chicken bones, or any other type of bone can be used to create an excellent broth.

The longer you simmer the broth, the better, that's why a crock pot is often used. Many people use filtered water, too.

**Good and Simple Bone Broth**

**Ingredients**

Bones (beef soup bones, chicken bones, etc.)
2 - 3 tablespoons raw Apple Cider Vinegar
Water

**Directions — Crock pot 1 hour on high; 24 hours on low**

Fill the crock pot with the bones. If you have bones with joints, that will add a lot of extra healthy gelatin to the broth.

Once the bones are in place, add enough water to completely cover the bones. I like to have one or two inches of water on top of the bones.

Add the apple cider vinegar.

Cover the crock pot and cook on high for about an hour. Then put it on low and allow the pot to cook for an additional 24 hours. (You can cook it longer but one full day should be enough.)

Remove the bones. You want to strain the broth and remove all meat and bones. Do NOT feed the bones to the dogs. Instead take them directly outside to prevent any dog pilfering and potential harm to your dog.

You now have a good, solid bone stock.

At this point, you can include additional ingredients such as kale, green beans, or broccoli to heighten the nutritional value of the broth but it's not necessary. Add them as soon as you turn off the crock pot. The vegetables will cook in the cooling broth.

Allow the broth to cool. You can refrigerate the broth at this point and you soon have a hard layer of fat on the top. You want to chip this off and throw it away. The broth underneath should have a gel texture. This is good for your dog's joints.

Note: If your broth hasn't gelled, then you may need more vinegar next time. Don't throw the non-gelled broth away; it is still packed with nutrients and good to use.

Store in labeled mason jars and refrigerate. If you don't think you will use all the broth right away, freeze it. You can also put the broth into an ice cube tray and give a cube as a treat to your dogs. Small dogs love this.

You can spoon tablespoons of the broth onto their daily food as a good way to make sure they have super nutritious food or include a tablespoon or two in a dog treat recipe. Your dog will appreciate it.

# NOTES

## 50 Dog Snack Recipes

*50 Dog Snack Recipes*

# INDEX

More Books in the Dog Training and Care Series ............... ii

**FOREWORD** ................................................................. 5
**ABOUT 50 DOG SNACK RECIPES** ................................. 7
**TABLE OF CONTENTS** ................................................. 11
**INTRODUCTION** ........................................................ 15
    A Word of Caution .................................................. 16
**HOLIDAY GIFT IDEAS USING TREAT JARS** .................. 17
    DIY Treat Jar Lids ................................................... 18
    Fun DIY Treat Bags ................................................. 18
    Quick DIY Dog Collar Treat Jar ............................... 19
    Super Easy DYI Dog Treat Jar ................................. 19
**HOLIDAY GIFT IDEAS USING WREATHS** ..................... 21
    DIY Easy Dog Biscuit Christmas Wreath ................ 23
    DIY Homemade Dog Bone Wreath ........................ 24
**BEWARE OF HIDDEN HOLIDAY DANGERS** .................. 27
    Poinsettias, Mistletoe, and Holly ........................... 27
    Christmas Cake, Mince Pies, and Christmas Pudding ........ 27
    Chocolate decorations, chocolate coins ................ 28
    Macadamia nuts and Walnuts ............................... 28
    Bones .................................................................... 29
    Alcohol ................................................................. 29
    What You Can Do .................................................. 29
**TIPS TO KEEP YOUR DOG SAFE DURING THE HOLIDAYS** ............... 30
**MAKING HOMEMADE DOG SNACKS** ........................ 31
    Three Golden Rules for Making Homemade Dog Treats ........ 35
    The Health Benefits of Homemade Dog Treats ..... 36
    How Many Treats Is Too Many? ............................. 36
**PREPARATION** .......................................................... 39
    Preparation and Storage Tips ................................ 39
    Kitchen Equipment List ......................................... 39

183

PREPARATION TIPS .................................................................. 39
BAKING TIPS ........................................................................... 40
DECORATING DOG BISCUITS AND COOKIES ............................... 41
DECORATING SHAPES AND CUTTERS ........................................ 41
BENEFITS OF DEHYDRATED DOG TREATS ................................... 42
   *How do you make dehydrated dog treats? ................... 43*
   *The handy oven method ................................................ 43*
   *The easy dehydrator method ......................................... 43*
   *Things to remember ...................................................... 44*
DETERMINING THE CORRECT SIZE TREAT ................................... 44
STORAGE TIPS ........................................................................ 44
HANDLING DOG FOOD – A FEW GENERAL TIPS .......................... 47

## SAFETY FIRST — BAD INGREDIENTS FOR DOGS .............. 49

   *Alcohol ........................................................................... 49*
   *Caffeine .......................................................................... 49*
   *Chocolate ....................................................................... 50*
   *Fatty Foods .................................................................... 50*
   *Fat Trimmings and Bones .............................................. 50*
   *Fruit Toxins .................................................................... 51*
   *Dairy Products and Milk ................................................ 51*
   *Mushrooms .................................................................... 52*
   *Nutmeg .......................................................................... 52*
   *Nuts ................................................................................ 52*
   *Garlic and Onions .......................................................... 52*
   *Baby Food ...................................................................... 53*
   *Cheese ............................................................................ 53*
   *Liver ............................................................................... 54*
   *Potatoes ......................................................................... 54*
   *Salt ................................................................................. 54*
   *Sugars and Sweeteners .................................................. 54*
   *Other potential dangers to avoid .................................. 55*
      Apple core pips — while the fruit of the apple is a wonderful treat for your dog, the seeds and core are not. ............................ 55
      Avocados ................................................................... 55
      Broccoli ..................................................................... 55
      Corn cobs .................................................................. 55
      Hops .......................................................................... 55
      Pear pips ................................................................... 55
      Plum kernels ............................................................. 55
      Potato skins .............................................................. 55
      Rhubarb .................................................................... 55

## 50 Dog Snack Recipes

Spoiled and moldy foods .................................................................. 55
Xylitol, a natural substance often used as a sugar substitute is highly toxic to dogs even in small amounts. .................................................. 55

**GOOD TREAT INGREDIENTS** ............................................................. 56

*Bananas* ................................................................................. 56
*Sweet Potato* ........................................................................... 57
*Flaxseeds* ............................................................................... 57
*Yogurt* ................................................................................... 57
*Salmon* .................................................................................. 58
*Nori* ..................................................................................... 58
*Blueberries* ............................................................................ 58
*Rosemary* .............................................................................. 58
*Pet-friendly Fruits* ................................................................... 58
MORE SAFE INGREDIENTS FOR HOMEMADE DOG TREATS ........................... 59

**CHRISTMAS & HOLIDAY HOMEMADE DOG SNACKS** .......................... 61

JINGLE BELLS HOLIDAY COOKIES .......................................................... 63
PEANUT BUTTER CHRISTMAS COOKIES .................................................. 64
BANANA CINNAMON CHRISTMAS CAKE ................................................. 65
HOLIDAY MERINGUE COOKIES FOR DOGS .............................................. 66
SWEET CINNAMON CHRISTMAS COOKIES ............................................... 67
BEEFY HOLIDAY BISCUITS .................................................................. 68
YOGURT-DIPPED GINGERBREAD DOG COOKIES ....................................... 70
CINNAMON APPLE CHRISTMAS CAKE .................................................... 72
CAROB-DIPPED CHRISTMAS COOKIES ................................................... 73
CAROB-DIPPED GINGERBREAD MEN ..................................................... 75
YOGURT-DIPPED CHRISTMAS COOKIES ................................................. 76
CHRISTMAS CHICKEN BISCUITS ........................................................... 78
NO COOK DOGGIE TRUFFLES GALORE ................................................... 79
PEANUT BUTTER MERINGUE COOKIES ................................................... 81

**CANINE COOKIES & PUPCAKES** ....................................................... 85

DELICIOUS CARROT CAKE PUPCAKES .................................................... 87
SUPER SPICED PUMPKIN PUPCAKES ..................................................... 88
DOGGIE DROOLIN' PEANUT BUTTER PUPCAKES ...................................... 90
QUICK AND EASY CHEWY CHICKEN COOKIES ......................................... 91
GOOD SCENT CINNAMON APPLE COOKIES ............................................. 92
FROSTING RECIPES FOR PUPCAKES ...................................................... 93
*Cinnamon Frosting* ................................................................... 93
*Carob Frosting* ........................................................................ 93

185

*Banana Carob Frosting* ............................................................... *93*
*Simple Egg Wash* ....................................................................... *94*

**FUN DOGGIE BISCUITS** ............................................................... **97**

    ALMOND BUTTER CAROB CHIP BISCUITS .................................................. 99
    CAROB-CHIP BISCUITS ................................................................ 101
    PEANUT BUTTER CAROB BISCUITS ...................................................... 102
    SOFT AND CHEWY BEEF BISCUITS ...................................................... 104
    PEANUT BUTTER FLAXSEED BISCUITS ................................................... 105
    PEANUT BUTTER AND OATS BISCUITS ................................................... 106
    FLAXSEED BISCUITS ................................................................... 108
    YOGURT-DIPPED PEANUT BUTTER BISCUITS ............................................. 110

**EXTRA SPECIAL DOG TREATS** ....................................................... **113**

    GINGERBREAD DOG TREATS ............................................................. 115
    CAROB-DIPPED PUMPKIN TREATS ....................................................... 116
    GLUTEN-FREE CAROB TREATS ........................................................... 118
    CANDIED YAM TREATS .................................................................. 119
    NO COOK PEANUT BUTTER YOGURT TREATS ........................................... 120
    BACON-FLAVORED DOG TREATS ......................................................... 122
    SWEET POTATO SOFTIES ................................................................ 123
    FROZEN YOGURT TREATS ................................................................ 124
    TASTY TUNA TREATS .................................................................... 125
    SUPER SIMPLE BEEF JERKY DOG TREATS ................................................ 126
    NO-BAKE CAROB-DIPPED YOGURT TREATS ............................................. 127
    GLUTEN-FREE PEANUT BUTTER CAROB TREATS ........................................ 128
    TURKEY JERKY DOG TREATS ............................................................. 130
    NO COOK EASY PB & C YOGURT TREATS ............................................... 131
    CAROB-DIPPED FROZEN PEANUT BUTTER TREATS ...................................... 132

**DOGGIE BITES AND STICKS** ........................................................ **135**

    SPICED BUTTERNUT SQUASH STICKS ................................................... 137
    PUMPKIN PEANUT BUTTER BITES ....................................................... 138
    SWEET POTATO STICKS ................................................................. 139
    PARMESAN ASIAGO CHEESE BITES ..................................................... 140
    CANDIED BEET BITES ................................................................... 142
    CHICKEN CHEDDAR BISCUIT BITES ..................................................... 143
    CHEDDAR PARMESAN BITES ............................................................ 144
    BACON CHEDDAR BISCUIT BITES ....................................................... 145
    CHEESY CHEDDAR BITES ................................................................ 146

**ALTERNATIVE TREATS AND INGREDIENTS** ............... 149
    ADDITIONAL HEALTHY TREAT IDEAS ....................................... 151
        *Carrots* ................................................................................. 151
        *Fresh Fruit* .......................................................................... 151
        *Plain, non-fat Yogurt* ......................................................... 151
        *Rice and Beef* ..................................................................... 151
        *Frozen Yogurt Pops* ........................................................... 152
        *Frozen Banana Pots* .......................................................... 152
        *Frozen Peanut Butter Pops* ............................................... 152
        *Cottage Cheese and Yogurt* .............................................. 152
        *Macaroni and Cheese* ....................................................... 152
    ALLERGIES AND SPECIAL DIETARY NEEDS ................................. 153
        *Wheat flour substitutes* .................................................... 153
        *Standard substitutions for wheat flour* ........................... 155
    BASIC HYPOALLERGENIC DOG TREAT RECIPE ........................... 157

**CONCLUSION** ............................................................... 159

**ENJOYED THIS BOOK?** ................................................. 161

**ABOUT THE AUTHOR** ................................................... 163

**ABOUT A LIFE WITH DOGS** .......................................... 163
        *Let's Connect!* ................................................................... 163

**MORE BOOKS BY THE AUTHOR** ................................... 165

**EXCERPT: BONDING WITH YOUR RESCUE DOG** ............ 167

**DISCLAIMER** ................................................................ 173

**APPENDIX A - WHEAT-FREE RECIPES** ........................... 175

**APPENDIX B — BONE BROTH RECIPE** ......................... 177
    GOOD AND SIMPLE BONE BROTH ........................................... 177

**NOTES** ........................................................................ 179

**INDEX** ......................................................................... 183

187

Made in the USA
Coppell, TX
30 January 2020